HARTLAND BRIDGE

OVER

St John River

PARISHES OF WAKEFIELD AND BRIGHTON

CARLETON CO., N. B.

Scale 20 ft to an inch

PUBLIC WORKS DEPARTMENT   FREDERICTON N.B. June 1920

WEST

SECTION THROUGH CD

DETAILS OF
REPOSITIONED SPANS ON NEW PIERS
Scale ½"=1'

DETAILS OF TEMPORARY SECTION X
Scale ½"=1'

SECTION EF THROUGH
TEMPORARY SPAN

SECTION NO.11.	SECTION NO.13	SECTION NO.15	SECTION NO.16	SECTION NO.17
197'.6"	144'.6"	144'.6"		51'.2"
REPOSITIONED HOWE TRUSS SPAN NO.2 THEN COVERED IN	NEW COVERED IN HOWE TRUSS SPAN SPAN NO.6	NEW COVERED IN HOWE TRUSS SPAN SPAN NO.7	WEST CONCRETE ABUTMENT	STONE EMBANKMENT

NO FASTER THAN A WALK

THE COVERED BRIDGES OF NEW BRUNSWICK

"Walk your horse or pay the fine!"

Stephen Gillis

Stephen Gillis & John Gillis

Cover: Keswick River No.7 (Burnside Haines), York Co. (standing): built in 1899, this bridge and the Nelson Hollow Bridge of Northumberland Co. are the only remaining New Brunswick bridges constructed in the nineteenth century that still stand. Note the diving board in the foreground and the beautifully clear water of the swimming hole.

Back Cover: Digdeguash River No.3 (McGuire), Charlotte Co. (standing).

Title page: Weldon Creek No.3 (Hartley Steeves-Dan Cupid Bridge), Albert Co. (standing): when this bridge was being built over Weldon Creek, the engineer in charge fell in love with a local girl and eventually married her. The bridge has been known as the "Dan Cupid Bridge" ever since. Look carefully beyond this bridge and you can see the Harris Steeves Bridge which spans Bull Creek.

Opposite: Smith Creek No.1 (Tranton), Kings Co. (standing).

Acknowledgments

During our research for *No Faster Than A Walk*, we enjoyed the opportunity to meet people and institutions with a common interest in covered bridges. There are many who have been very helpful and we are especially thankful to the following: Deborah Gillis, Mrs Della Webster (nee Gorham), Mr Donald Rideout, Mr Austin Renton, Mr James Neales, Mr Wallace Cook, Mr Ron Badger, Mr and Mrs Robert Barr, Mr R.A. Malloy, The Saint Croix Courier, The Calais Free Library, The Daily Gleaner, The Old Manse Library, The Public Archives of New Brunswick, The New Brunswick Department of Transportation, The National Archives of Canada, Saint Stephen Public Library, Goose Lane Editions.

Published by Goose Lane Editions Ltd., 248 Brunswick Street, Fredericton, New Brunswick, Canada, E3B 1G9, with the assistance of the Canada Council, the New Brunswick Department of Education, the New Brunswick Department of Tourism, Recreation & Heritage, and the University of New Brunswick, 1988.

Book design by Julie Scriver

Canadian Cataloguing in Publication Data

Gillis, Stephen, 1951
   No faster than a walk

Bibliography: p.95
includes index.

1. Covered bridges — New Brunswick.
2. New Brunswick — Description and travel — Views.   I. Gillis, John, 1957-.   II. Title.

TG27.N4G54 1988   624'.37   C88-098546-1

ISBN 0-86492-091-1

Illustrations appear courtesy of the following (credit abbreviations appear in brackets):

Bonnie & James Bishop (Bishop)
The Daily Gleaner, Fredericton
E.F. Gillis
National Film Board of Canada (NFB)
New Brunswick Department of Transportation (N.B. Dept. of Transportation)
Provincial Archives of New Brunswick (PANB)
Public Archives of Canada (PAC)
Saint Thomas Parish, Red Bank
Tennesea & Irene Schwetz (Schwetz)
Mrs M. Tozer

Graphic illustrations by Dan Daigle
Photographs appearing without a credit were taken by the authors.

This book is dedicated to the Chief Bridge
Engineers of the Bridge Department,
Department of Transportation, Province of
New Brunswick.

A.R. Wetmore, Chief Bridge Engineer,
1894-1925
C.A. MacVey, Chief Bridge Engineer,
1925-1951
R.A. Malloy, Chief Bridge Engineer,
1951-1955
B.H. Hagerman, Chief Bridge Engineer,
1955-1966

Preface

The sound of a vehicle crossing a covered bridge is unique. The initial, hollow impact of tires is followed by a rattling of the floor boards. Beneath the bridge it sounds as though the flooring is not nailed down, as though the stress will bounce the planking off the stringers. Each timber takes its turn and the progress of the unseen vehicle can be followed along the bridge. The old structure becomes a sound-chamber, resonating with the traffic.

Why do we start with a sound? Perhaps it is nostalgia for those lost days of childhood, down by the creek, sheltering from summer rain under the bridge.

The covered bridges of the province of New Brunswick are in the last decades of their lives and we realized that many of them would not last very much longer. There was a sense of urgency about our project; indeed, most of the existing bridges were built in the early part of this century.

We found conflicting dates and facts as we searched through old files and newspaper reports. Much of our information was based upon the memories of those who grew up during the golden age of the bridges, before the Second World War, and memory is not always reliable. However, the purpose of this book is not to offer the last word on the subject, but to try to capture the sentiments aroused by the province's "kissing bridges."

Even our measurements remain fixed in New Brunswick's past, for they follow the Imperial system rather than Metric. The old bridges were built in feet and yards and it seemed only proper to maintain those standards.

There are 73 standing bridges, and photographs of all of them are contained in this book. This number includes those bridges under the care of the federal government in Fundy National Park and those bridges built or maintained by the province of New Brunswick. We did not include private bridges built especially for tourism: the only exception being the Magnetic Hill Bridge (which is the property of the city of Moncton), which was relocated from the Coverdale River where it was originally constructed by the provincial government.

Below: Rusagonis River No.2 (Patrick Owen), Sunbury Co. (standing) (see photo p.6).

Photographs of many bridges no longer standing are also presented, as a partial record of the earlier covered bridge heritage. Several people generously allowed us to use their treasured images and in doing so greatly enhanced our record. Two principles guided our decision to include some of these no-longer standing bridges. In some cases there are special features of construction which add to our knowledge of bridge-building technique, while in others the historical associations seemed compelling.

BRIDGE NOTICE.

SEALED TENDERS, MARKED

"TENDERS FOR STILLWATER BRIDGE,"

will be received at the Department of Public Works, Fredericton, until

FRIDAY,

10th February next, at noon,

for rebuilding the Stillwater Bridge, Digdeguash River, St. Patrick, Charlotte Co., according to Plan and Specification to be seen at said Department, and at the Office of Mitchell & Stevens, St. Stephen.

Each tender must be accompanied by a certified Bank Cheque, or Cash for an amount equal to 5 per cent. of the tender, which will be forfeited if the party called upon declines to enter into contract. If the tender be not accepted, the deposit will be returned. Two good sureties must be named in the tender.

The lowest or any tender not necessarily accepted.

P. G. RYAN,
Chief Commissioner.

Department Public Works,
Fredericton, January 26, 1888

PANB

Right: Rusagonis River No.2 (Patrick Owen), Sunbury Co. (standing): this photograph shows a special bridge and a very special person. The bridge has an unusual window running almost its entire length. The man in the foreground is C.A. MacVey, the Bridge Engineer for the Bridge Department from 1925 to 1951.

The Daily Gleaner

Above: Lower Forty-Five No.1, Albert Co. (standing): this bridge is within the boundaries of Fundy National Park and is therefore in the care of the federal government. The bridge sits amid the tree tops over a steep canyon.

Right: Tynemouth Creek (Mouth), Saint John Co. (standing).

Foreword

There were four Chief Bridge Engineers in the history of the Bridge Department. The position was renamed as Director of Structures after the Bridge Department was amalgamated with the Highways Department in 1966.

The first Chief Bridge Engineer was Andrew R. Wetmore. Mr Wetmore was a graduate of the Royal Military College in Kingston, Ontario. He was employed by the Canadian Pacific Railway before coming to New Brunswick, where he served as the Chief Bridge Engineer for the years 1894 to 1925.

The province built several steel structures under Mr Wetmore's supervision. During the construction of the Gunningsville Bridge at Moncton, the crews were working on the river bottom in a pressure-filled chamber. Mr Wetmore arrived on the scene and wanted to inspect the work at the bottom of the chamber. His party entered the air-lock and the crew had only introduced 10 lbs of compressed air when Mr Wetmore complained of pain in his ears. He left the chamber and walked around the field for a few minutes before trying again. Eventually the Chief Bridge Engineer's tolerance was built up until he was able to descend to the work area. When he finally arrived, they couldn't get him to leave. Such was the level of the man's professional interest.

Mr Wetmore was followed in 1925 by Mr C. Andrew MacVey. Mr MacVey was born in Bloomfield, Kings Co.. He attended the

University of New Brunswick before becoming the Chief Bridge Engineer for twenty-six years. During his term as C.B.E., the wooden bridge was considered the most practical way of spanning a river. Other building materials were becoming more fashionable but they did not capture Mr MacVey's interest. It was said C.A. MacVey was totally dedicated to his work and had little tolerance for anyone who was not.

Mr Richard A. Malloy was a graduate of the University of New Brunswick and served as the Chief Bridge Engineer from 1951 to 1955. Mr Malloy was noted for his interest in promoting native stone as a building material. He favored the granite-faced, rigid frame design for small bridges. Stone Bridge in the north end of Fredericton was one of Mr Malloy's creations. He also built the charming bridge over the New River in Charlotte Co..

The last Chief Bridge Engineer was Mr Bernard H. Hagerman. He served in the position from 1955 to 1966. Among the noteworthy projects Mr Hagerman devised and built was a bridge design that became known as the "arched T-beam." He had no previous research to rely on and this type of span had not been built before. Soon after the arch was completed, Mr Hagerman was asked if the bridge was ready to take the strain of a large piece of equipment that had to be moved to the opposite side. He replied that the bridge might as well be put to the test now as later and instructed the machine be moved. The bridge is still in use today in the Mactaquac area.

R.B. Malloy

Mr R.B. Malloy served as Director of Structures for the Department of Transportation until his retirement. He is the son of Mr R.A. Malloy, Chief Bridge Engineer from 1951 to 1955.

Above: South Oromocto River No.3 (Bell), Sunbury Co. (standing).

Below: Odellach River No.2 (Tomlinson Mill), Victoria Co. (standing).

Above: North Branch Bridge, Northumberland Co. (not standing): this old bridge was located on the Plaster Rock-Renous Highway. Note the unusual design of the face of the bridge, the work of the local Bridge Superintendent.

Man has always been a wanderer. From the dawn of human history he has travelled and influenced the face of his known world. In travelling he has crossed the streams and open spaces lying in his way.

The first bridge was probably nothing more than a fallen tree or a raft of ice which served the limited purpose of reaching the other side. Such accidents of nature were in time succeeded by conscious human design. Men built their own simple bridges.

It was when the arch was developed, however, that true bridge architecture was born. Long before the birth of Christ, early builders, employing the arch, were able to construct impressive structures. The first covered bridges were apparently erected in Medieval Europe. Among the earliest examples were those built in Lucerne, Switzerland. These two fourteenth-century bridges—one bearing the ominous name of "Dance of Death Bridge," after the painting which adorned its ceiling—were the first to make use of the truss, an essential item in the subsequent development of building techniques.

The *Ponte Vecchio* or "Old Bridge" was constructed in Florence, Italy, at about the same time as the Swiss bridges. This famous old bridge, which was lined on both sides with jewelry shops, is still standing today.

In the late sixteenth century the *Rialto* covered bridge was built in Venice. This was a truly remarkable structure. Like the *Ponte Vecchio* its sides were lined with shops and its centre was built high enough to allow the passage of barges.

The mechanics of the truss were not fully understood in the early days of its use. It did, however, allow for the extensive use of wood as a building material and exploited the magic of the triangle. A triangle cannot

be distorted; when stressed it will resist until broken, while a rectangle is less rigid and is easily deviated.

The "king post" was a truss of great strength but of rather short span. It was of little use in crossing any real distance. By placing a triangle at either end of a rectangle, the entire structure became stable and could extend for a considerable length. It then became known as a "queen" truss.

The mechanics of the truss were first explained by Andrea Palladio in his famous work entitled *A Treatise on Architecture.* In his *Treatise,* the Venetian Palladio described four variations of the truss design.

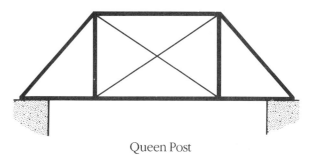

Queen Post

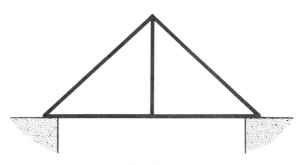

King Post

Above: East Branch St. Nicholas River No. 1, Kent Co. (standing).

Right: Hammond River No.3 (Smithtown), Kings Co. (standing): under this bridge lies a fine salmon pool. More than one angler has wiled away the time counting the flies hooked to the bottom chords, victims of the strong updraft found under the bridge when the wind blows.

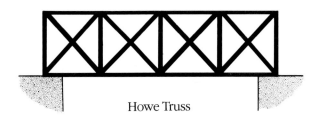

Howe Truss

Towne Lattice

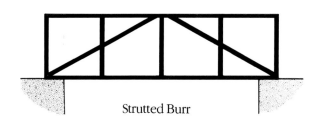

Strutted Burr

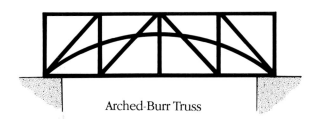

Arched-Burr Truss

Some historians suggest the 1742 English translation of Palladio's work led to the beginning of wooden truss construction in North America. Several American builders, who may have been influenced by Palladio, patented their own variations of the wooden truss at about this time.

Theodore Burr improved the King post truss by adding an arch. This design was popular in New England and there are several standing bridges in New Brunswick employing this pattern today.

Up-Set End

Ithiel Town developed an unusual truss which consisted of timbers pegged together to form a lattice work. It was an extremely simple truss and was described as being "built by the mile and sold by the yard." Town patented his design in 1820 and prospered nicely from the royalties. There are, however, no standing covered bridges of this design left in New Brunswick.

William Howe, yet another American, supplemented the wooden truss by the employment of steel rods. Perhaps this was the precursor of the eventual domination of steel over wood in bridge design. A bridge built with the Howe Truss could be adjusted on a regular basis simply by tightening or loosening the rods, thus ensuring maximum strength. The ends of each rod were swollen at the point where the thread was to be engraved, meaning the rod would not be weakened by the process of cutting in the thread. This was called an "up-set end." The vast majority of the surviving bridges in New Brunswick today are of the Howe Truss design.

Familiarity with the covered bridge and knowledge of the efficiency of the wooden truss may well have been imported in to New Brunswick with the arrival of the United Empire Loyalists in the 1780s. Certainly, by the early nineteenth century there was an increase in prosperity and population in the province, which meant new roads and therefore new bridges. It was during this period that the covered bridge became unmistakeably part of the landscape.

Right: Shepody River No.3 (Germantown Lake), Albert Co. (standing).

Below: Petitcodiac River No.3 (Hasty), Westmorland Co. (standing).

St. Croix Courier

Above: Old Covered Bridge, Charlotte Co. (not standing): this bridge spanned the St. Croix River from St. Stephen to Calais, Maine. International covered bridges were extremely rare, although St. Stephen seems to have had more than one. This old covered bridge was also called the Ferry Point Bridge; it was built in 1827 and dismantled in 1894. At one time The Greatest Show on Earth, the famous circus of P.T. Barnum, visited St. Stephen. After a successful performance the circus moved on to its next engagement in Calais, Maine. Jumbo, the gigantic and world-famous elephant, led the parade across the Old Covered Bridge to the American side.

PANB

From the beginning the building of a bridge was a costly venture and public money was not always available. If the distance to be spanned was small, the cost of the bridge might be borne by a single mill-owner or the operator of a lumber firm. The larger structures were not so easily financed. On occasion a bridge company would be founded, whereby a group of local businessmen would bind together and sponsor the construction of a bridge. To regain their investment they would charge a toll upon every person using the crossing. The authority to collect these tolls was granted by the Legislature of the Province of New Brunswick.

In 1845, an Act of the Legislature made the following declaration concerning tolls to be charged by the newly formed Saint Croix Bridge Corporation:

> For each Foot Passenger, one penny half penny; One Person and Horse, two penny half penny; A Horse and Cart or Wagon, four pence; A Horse and Sleigh or Chaise, or other pleasure Carriage drawn by one Horse, six pence ... Sheep and Swine, one half penny each; And to each Team one person only shall be allowed, as driver, to pass free of toll.

Left: Foot bridge, Doaktown, Northumberland Co. (not standing).

13

Speed on the covered bridges was strictly governed. The previously mentioned Act also carried the following warning:

> And be it enacted, that no Horse or other Beast, or Carriage of any kind, shall be taken over the said Bridge *at a pace faster than a walk on pain of forfeiture of twenty shillings for every offence*, to be recovered in an action of debt before any Justice of the Peace, on complaint of the Toll Gatherer ... the said money, when recovered, to be applied to the use of the said Corporation.

In 1944 the province had 320 covered bridges.

The longest covered bridge, at Hartland, is 1,282 feet in length.

The last surviving "hip" or "cottage" roofs are those of Nelson Hollow, Northumberland Co., and Turtle Creek No.4, Peter Jonah, Albert Co.

Above: Nackawic River No.5 (Nackawic Siding), York Co. (standing).

Above: Gaspereau River No.2 (Burpee), Queens Co. (standing): the Burpee spans the Gaspereau River east of Chipman. This early photograph shows the bridge in beautiful condition although signs of old age are all-too present today. The bridge was named in honour of a family which lived nearby.

Below: Smith Creek No.5 (Oldfield), Kings Co. (standing): this bridge can be found spanning Smith Creek at Newtown. Built in 1910, the bridge was named after a local mill-owner.

Why would the movement of a single horse over a wooden bridge, built to withstand tons, be such a grave offence? Would it matter if the horse ran or walked? He would surely have the same mass. On February 26th, 1889, Mr Alfred Haines, an engineer and Inspector of Bridges, wrote as follows to The Honourable P.G. Ryan, Chief Commissioner of Bridges. (The letter is printed as written.)

> I consider a truss in pretty good condition and will carry a load from 15 to 20 tons safely when the truss will stand the motion and vibration that a trotting horse of 800 lbs. will put it in. I consider it safer to trot a horse on an old truss than a new truss, on account of their being more elasticity or spring to the new timber than the old, and is not so apt to trip the lateral braces in the old truss as in a truss of new timber, on account of the elasticity in the timber … I have mended a number of trusses that have been broken by trotting horses over them. If the people would consider the damage and the danger that there is in trotting horses over a bridge, and stop doing so, it would add from five to ten years to the life of a bridge.

The trotting of a horse would set in motion a regular vibration within the bridge span. Anyone who has stood on a cable footbridge will recognize the wave generated by the movement of another person on the bridge. When an army is on the march the pace is broken and the soldiers cross a wooden bridge with normal stride to prevent damage.

The destructiveness of this regular vibration has been a hard lesson to bridge designers. In recent years a multi-million dollar suspension bridge, the Tacoma

Narrows Bridge over Puget Sound, rocked-and-rolled to its end as a result of high winds and what some said was a basic engineering mistake. Meanwhile, many of New Brunswick's bridges still sport a sign warning: "WALK YOUR HORSE OR PAY THE FINE, $20.00!"

Time passed and transportation modes evolved. The advent of the automobile made it necessary to amend the speed regulations on the province's bridges. The Motor Vehicle Law, 1926, read:

> If a motor vehicle ... is operated at a rate of speed greater than one mile in four minutes, it shall be deemed *prima facie* to be operated at a rate of speed greater than is reasonable and proper and in violation of this section.

One mile in four minutes means 15 miles per hour or 38 kilometers per hour. The legislators were maintaining their caution.

Incidentally, the same piece of legislation states that the operator of a motor vehicle, upon meeting a horse on the road, must come to an immediate stop for as long as is reasonable to allow the animal or animals to pass. Motor vehicles must also turn to the right of the centre of the roadway to allow oncoming traffic to pass safely. In 1926 traffic was legally required to travel on the right-hand side of the roadway. (It has been claimed that the custom of vehicles travelling on the right side of the road was the result of complaints from American tourists who encountered road hazards while venturing through New Brunswick!)

Above: Tantramar River No.2 (Wheaton), Westmorland Co. (standing): this bridge spans the Tantramar River on the High Marsh Road.

Building a new bridge meant, of course, the acquisition of land. A design was chosen to fit the site and tenders were called. A respondent to the tender was required to submit a complete bid along with a certified cheque or cash to the amount of 10% of the total bid. Calls for tenders were posted about the province and responses were opened by the Minister of the Bridge Department with his Deputy Minister.

The lowest tender was not always accepted, for the Department would look very carefully at the experience of the would-be builder as well as his financial situation. If the builder's previous projects were sub-standard, or if the Department felt that the builder was not financially secure, the tender would be awarded to a more qualified person.

One of the most active of New Brunswick's bridge builders early in this century was Albert E. Smye of Alma, Albert County. Smye also constructed wharves, piers, and warehouses, as his letter-head (reproduced here) makes plain.

Above: Coverdale River No.2 (John Mitton), Albert Co. (not standing): this bridge was built by A.E. Smye of Albert Co.

Right: Letterhead used by A.E. Smye

ALBERT E. SMYE CONTRACTOR
ALMA, ALBERT CO., N.B.

CONTRACTS MADE
— FOR —
CONSTRUCTION
-- OF --
WHARF AND BRIDGE
PIERS,
WAREHOUSES,
BRIDGES,
ETC.

CORRESPONDENCE
SOLICITED.

In 1907 tenders were called for the construction of the Saw Mill Creek Bridge, Parish of Hopewell, Albert Co.. There were three builders who responded:

Tenders for Saw Mill Creek Bridge

No.	Name of Tenderer	Amount	Deposit.
1	A.E. Smye	$2,974.00	$149.00
2	Whitman Bros.	$3,060.00	$155.00
3	W.R. Fawcett	$4,500.00	nil

Opened Sept. 3rd, 1907.
by T.B. Winslow & P. Hughes

The successful tender was submitted by A.E. Smye and the bridge was built the following year.

BRIDGE NOTICE

SEALED TENDERS MARKED

Tender for Saw Mill Creek Bridge

will be received at the Department of Public Works, Fredericton, until

MONDAY,

2nd day of September, 1907, at noon,

For rebuilding Saw Mill Creek Bridge, Parish of Hopewell, Albert Co., according to Plan and Specification to be seen at the Public Works Department, Fredericton, N. B., at the office of Hon. C. J. Osman, M. P. P., Hillsboro, N. B., and at the residence of Mr. S. S. Ryan, M. P. P., Coverdale, Albert Co., N. B.

Each tender must be accompanied by a certified Bank Cheque or Cash, for an amount equal to five per cent of the tender, which will be forfeited if the party tendering declines to enter into contract when called upon. Should the tender be not accepted the deposit will be returned. Two good sureties must be named in each tender. Not obliged to accept lowest or any tender.

Department Public Works,
Fredericton, August 19th, 1907

C. H. LaBILLOIS,
Chief Commissioner

PANB

Below right: Saw Mill Creek No.1, Albert Co. (standing): this bridge is closed to traffic but is preserved as a part of the local heritage. It was built in 1905 by A.E. Smye.

Above: Meanen Cove Bridge, Kings Co. (not standing): this bridge had to be replaced when the local fire department refused to allow their tanker truck to cross the old structure.

Right: Vaughan Creek No.1 (Irish River), Saint John Co. (standing): these two bridges are at St. Martins. In the background is Vaughan Creek No.2 (Hardscrabble). Note the recent addition of a sidewalk to the Irish River Bridge. The bridges needed reinforcement, so the Department of Highways installed the steel girders seen under the structure.

On numerous occasions the Department of Public Works has had to face the dilemma of what to do with an ageing covered bridge. On the one hand is the desire to preserve part of our rural heritage, an historic link to the past, while the increasing demands being placed on bridges, covered or not, by growing traffic and heavier loads, make changes urgent.

The Department has attempted to upgrade the old wooden bridges with reinforcement and various structural improvements. At the same time, most of the open-faced abutments have been replaced with reinforced concrete. Sometimes steel has been used to augment the wooden bottom chords of the bridge itself. But such measures were not always possible. Many times there was little or nothing that could be done to solve the problem of an old bridge faced with modern requirements.

The Meanen Cove Bridge, Kings Co., was a good case in point. The rate of growth on the far side of the bridge was dramatic when several subdivisions sprang up along the Model Farm Road and beyond, multiplying the traffic. The end was in sight for the bridge when the Rothesay Fire Department refused to allow their tanker trucks to cross the structure. The combined weight of a truck and its load of water would undoubtedly have been too much for the aged timbers to withstand. The only available route for the fire department, in an emergency, was a lengthy detour round the bridge. The community could not afford to gamble with life and property so the bridge was replaced with a reinforced concrete span.

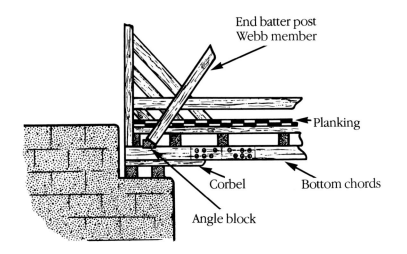

End batter post
Webb member

Planking

Bottom chords

Corbel

Angle block

Left: Construction detail

Right: Detail from Cocagne River No.3 (Poirier), Westmorland Co. (standing): this bridge is on its last legs. It is forbidden to all traffic and has been stripped of most of its siding. The photograph illustrates well the details of a Howe Truss. Note the metal rods between the beams. These rods enabled the Bridge Supervisors to "true up" the span as required.

The province's engineers have elected to save covered bridges whenever possible. When a bridge is structurally sound yet cannot meet the contemporary demands of the community, it is dismantled systematically. Each piece is numbered and recorded. Later the bridge may be reassembled at a site where less stress will be put upon it. The Magnetic Hill Covered Bridge is an example of such a transplant—although in this case the bridge was rebuilt by the City of Moncton to enhance a tourist attraction.

In some instances (Moosehorn Creek Bridge, Kings Co.; Sawmill Creek No.1, Albert Co.; Little Lepreau River No.1, Charlotte Co.) bridges were moved a few yards to a retirement location or the new road was reconstructed nearby. There they remain part of the community without hampering future growth. The relocated bridges serve as tourist attractions and add greatly to the unique flavour of New Brunswick while new reinforced concrete bridges answer the traffic problems.

Above: Little Lepreau (Mill Pond), Charlotte Co. (standing): this bridge is now a tourist attraction. It has just been relocated a few yards from its original location at a cost of approximately $50,000.

Left: Moosehorn Covered Bridge, Kings Co. (standing): this bridge was refurbished by The League For Rural Renewal under the supervision of James Neales of Kings Co. The Department of Transportation wanted to replace the missing boards with new lumber but Mr Neales insisted that aged boards be found, whereupon the Department bought boards from an old barn nearby and so the bridge maintained its weathered look.

The keeping of public accounts was serious business at the turn of this century—not to suggest that it is of any less importance today! For the building of a bridge, those in charge were required to account for every last penny, every nail, board, tool, and wage paid. There was little or no mercy for the man who was not "worth his salt."

On one occasion, on the death of the Bridge Superintendent of Gloucester Co. the Chief Bridge Engineer, Mr C.A. MacVey, was obliged to write thus to the daughter of the deceased:

> Your late father had been supplied by the Department with a quantity of tools, such as sledges, cross cut saw, ¾ inch auger, ⅝ inch ship auger, claw hammers, hand saw, several peavies and shovels, three or four picks, etc.
>
> I would ask you to have these gathered together and when ready notify Mr Losier, the newly appointed bridge superintendent, to call and get them. (Oct. 2nd, 1941)

Little was taken for granted. Instructions to newly appointed Bridge Supervisors included the following: "It will be necessary for you to exercise every care in the way of economy and in seeing to it that each man does an honest day's work."

Below: Kennebecasis River No.23 (Malone), Kings Co. (standing): the Malone is still as picturesque as it appears in this turn-of-the century photograph. Those familiar with the vast waters of the lower Kennebecasis may be surprised to see the size of the river this far inland. The bridge is off the usually beaten track on the Goshen Road.

PANB

Left: The ends of the bridges were almost always boxed in to lessen the effects of weather on the truss-work resting on the abutments. A few of these covers were also boarded in on top to prevent the accumulation of litter and toward off cigarette butts.

Above: Note the stacked shell rock and reinforced concrete combination in this abutment.

Left: Kennebecasis River No.9 (Plumweseep), Kings Co. (standing): the bridge was built in 1910, a few years before this photograph was taken. The trees have since grown very tall and this clear view of the bridge is not possible today.

Above: Name unknown, Nashwaak River, York Co (not standing): the bridge could not take the added pressure of the pulp wood piled against its piers. The title of the photograph is *Jam of logs in the Nashwaak River.*

Right: Millstream No.5 (Centreville), Kings Co. (standing): spans the Millstream on the Pleasant Ridge Road.

24

Bridge building, like almost any governmental activity, was not free from the gentle tug of the politician's hand.

Members of the Legislative Assembly, both those in power and those in the opposition, were forces to be dealt with when decisions about bridge construction were to be made. In the "hungry thirties" government was the largest and, indeed, in many communities the only employer. The building of a bridge was often regarded as a "make-work project" for the men of families in greatest need. Whether a man was hired or not, however, often depended on his political leaning.

Below: Rolling Dam, Charlotte Co. (not standing): this bridge stood on the Digdeguash River.

Schwetz

Each county had a local committee of supporters of the government—that is, of the particular political party in power at that time. It was this local committee which approved of the men to be granted employment. If the members of the committee were not entirely satisfied with the choice of workers, a complaint was passed on to their "member," who put things in order without delay.

In a letter from the Deputy Minister of the Bridge Department dated September 27, 1937, we find a fairly clear indication of the Government's opinion of patronage:

> The custom in the Department for years ... has been for the Foreman to interview the local Member (of the Legislature), if possible, and get his idea as to which one of the Committee men he should go to for labour when work is being carried on. This is purely a matter of patronage and it has always been done without any expense to the Department.

Other examples from that same year illustrate the system at work. The Minister of Public Works, A.A. Dysart, who was also the Premier of the province, received a letter from a man dismissed from work on the Upper Jemseg Bridge, Queens Co. This had occurred because two men in charge of the work claimed that he had not voted for them as councillors in a recent election. Meanwhile, three men were dismissed from work at the McCann Bridge at Rollingdam in Charlotte Co. because they were not agreeable to the committee. We can only speculate on the number of "political" jobs the covered bridges of New Brunswick have maintained throughout their long history.

With the appearance of the motor vehicle on the roads of the province, the covered bridges began to show their age. It was not simply a matter of speed and the frequency of traffic. They were not prepared for the onslaught of trucks and other heavy machinery.

On September 2nd, 1918, a Saint John man wrote to the Department of Public Works complaining about an accident where his truck had fallen through the bottom of one of the province's covered bridges, and sought damages for the government's failure to maintain the structure adequately. He argued as follows:

> On examination of this bridge, I found that the stringers were rotten, so rotten that I could pull them to pieces with my hands. I don't think that it will be any trouble to prove this bridge was in bad condition and not safe for people to travel over as I believe the stringers to be still on the side of the bank.
>
> In regard to my car being overloaded, the Government itself purchased trucks which have a carrying capacity of five tons, and how does the Government expect these trucks to go over the highways if the bridges will not carry them.

Note the reference to the vehicle in question as a "car." Now for the rebuttal, the response from the Minister of Public Works:

> I note what you say about the condition of the bridge at the time, also as to your car being overloaded, and that you use the excuse for overloading your car, the fact that the Government has purchased trucks which have a capacity of five tons, and you inquire, "How does the government expect these trucks to go over the highways if the bridges will not carry them?" In reply I beg to say that

Above: Becaguimec River No.3 (Mangrum), Carleton Co. (standing): the loose piled rock was called "riprap." This type of abutment was referred to as open-faced cribwork.

Left: Mill Creek Bridge, Location Unknown (not standing): there must have been a large amount of stone in the nearby fields. It would not have been economical to transport this material any distance.

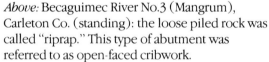

Above: The Cain Bridge, Kings Co. (not standing): the sign on the bridge reads "Cain Bridge—1913 $20.00 fine for driving faster than a walk on this bridge." If you look carefully you can see the photographer's horse at the entrance of the bridge.

Right: Darlings Island, Kings Co. (standing): this is the only way to reach Darlings Island by car. In recent years a number of expensive homes have been built on the island. How long will the old bridge hold-up to the increasing traffic while also coping with the tremendous loads of modern fire and snow removal equipment?

while it is true that we have certain trucks of five ton capacity, we do not allow them to go over even our best bridges without reinforcing these bridges to carry such weight. You can readily see by this that your excuse for overloading your truck does not hold good. You admit that you had 3,000 weight on your truck, and that most farmers carry a weight of 3,000 in their cars when coming to the city, but, you forget to take into consideration the weight of your truck which adds to the 3,000 weight you had on, it would mean no less than three or four tons. This fact convinces me that you never took into consideration what weight would be safely carried over any of the bridges of this province. Further, this bridge was known to others, and may have been known to you, to have been in a weakened condition, and yet, notwithstanding this you took the risk to pass over it with practically from three to four tons.

Those of us heading to market with our overloaded cars had better beware of such calculating logic!

The approaches to the bridges were frequently very sharp and the older bridges were built "square to the river." This represented the least expensive way to build and was not a problem to the slow, animal-drawn vehicles of the day. The automobile was neither as patient nor as slow, making the sharp turns to many of the bridges a real menace. Some of the roads, or at least their approachways, were rebuilt to accommodate the increased speed. After a particularly close call in Queens Co., in 1937, the Chief Bridge Engineer demonstrated his impatience with the new mode of transportation as follows:

> I am enclosing herein a letter ... concerning a bad turn in the end of the road at the Burpee Bridge. I have never been in a position to afford an eight cylinder car but was always under the impression that they had more than one gear shift and that in any dangerous place, such as this man described, a second or low gear was used on any car.

Some bridges were in locations where it was impractical to straighten the road. The terrain may have been of solid rock or the lie of the land made the characteristic "s" turn unavoidable.

Many of the standing bridges have been badly damaged by large pulp trucks which carry a boom or mechanical arm resting on top of the load of pulpwood. On more than one occasion these booms have torn out the upper woodwork of the crossbeams. The government has responded to the situation by installing metal barricades a few meters from each end of the bridge. If a loaded truck can clear the barricades than it can safely pass through the bridge.

Building or repairing a bridge was a multi-skilled endeavour. Though experience was required in many trades, the work was

Above: Trout Creek No.5 (Moores Mill), Kings Co. (standing): this bridge spans the Trout Creek on the Drummond Road.

usually done by a few, hard-working labourers—and there was always the Bridge Supervisor to look over the shoulders of the crew. So it should be, for it was the Supervisor's head on the line. Yet the crew had to be masons, carpenters and engineers. The men who built the bridges were familiar with barn construction, the joints and cuts employed were common to both structures.

There was little variation in the straightforward design of the bridges. As long as the end of the bridge was wide and high enough to accommodate a wagon fully loaded with hay, it met local requirements. The best opportunity for originality in bridge construction was in the design of the roof, yet there are only two bridges standing in New Brunswick which have the unusual "cottage" or "hip" roof (Nelson Hollow in Northumberland Co. and Peter Jonah in Albert Co.).

Above left: The Connors Bridge, Queens Co. (not standing): ice or lumber has damaged this bridge during the high waters of spring. Note the uncovered Howe Truss in the background.

Left: Turtle Creek No.4 (Peter Jonah), Albert Co. (standing): this is one of two New Brunswick bridges having a "Hip or Cottage" roof. The metal barrier at the entrance of the bridge is to prevent trucks with high loads from ripping out the top of the span. This bridge was almost demolished in the early eighties but for the prompt action of local residents and the Albert County Historical Society.

29

Mill Brook No.1 (Nelson Hollow), Northumberland Co. (standing): there used to be scores of covered bridges in Northumberland Co., spanning rivers and streams from Miramichi Bay to the headwaters. Built in the 1870s and renovated in 1899, the Nelson Hollow is the last bridge standing in this area. The bridge was closed to traffic in 1938 with the construction of the steel bridge nearby. It was restored by the Doaktown Historical Society in 1977. This bridge is one of two remaining bridges built in the nineteenth century and is probably the oldest standing covered bridge in the province (see detail 3, p.59). The province's other old-timer is the Burnside Haines in York Co., built in 1899 (see cover photo).

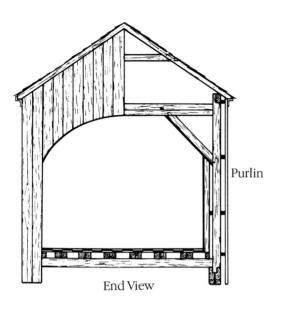

Purlin

End View

After the turn of this century, most of the bridges built used imported timbers from the Pacific Coast. Large beams of douglas fir were brought in from British Columbia. There was an extensive supply and we can only assume the cost of transportation must have been relatively cheap.

Douglas fir is an exceptionally strong building material and resistant to rot. It was much preferred to native species for the construction of the bridge chords. Most of New Brunswick's white pine was felled during the feverish days of shipbuilding in the previous century and very large timbers were now in short supply from within the province. One of the most frequent suppliers of the giant beams from B.C. was the Robertson and Hackett Sawmill Co. Ltd. of Vancouver.

New Brunswick trees were not entirely ignored in bridge building, however, and only the very large "chords" were imported. The choice flooring material was good old N.B. black spruce. It was well known to resist rot better than other conifers. Hemlock was abundant but deemed too weak and receptive to decay for use in construction of the floors or carrying beams; it was, nevertheless, used to fashion the angle blocks. These angle blocks allowed the diagonals to sit square to the load. The square cut also reduced the extent of the end of the beam exposed to the elements, thus limiting decay.

The sides of the bridge were boarded in with whatever wood was plentiful, mostly hemlock, while the preferred choice for the roofing was cedar shingles. The natural chemicals in cedar were effective preservatives and would protect the bridge for decades. Cedar was also used for "horsebacks." These were usually temporary reinforcements put under the bridge to shore it up until time was available for more permanent repairs. Whenever a Town Truss was employed (rarely in New Brunswick) oak pegs were used to fasten the timbers together. In the late forties chemically treated hardwoods replaced black spruce in the construction of the floors and maple or yellow birch was generally employed. Beech was not acceptable, as it would not absorb creosote, a wood preservative.

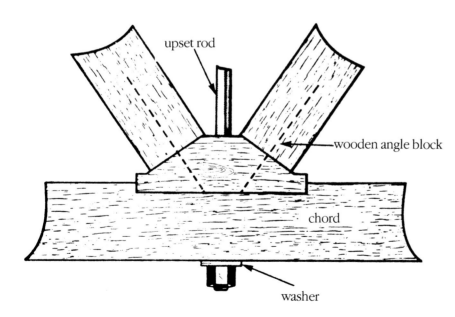

upset rod

wooden angle block

chord

washer

Right: Ship knees were made from the trunk and root of an elm tree (see diagram p.33). This picture shows the modern version of an old idea.

Above: Canaan River No.1 (Clark Aaron), Queens Co. (standing): this bridge spans the Canaan River on the South Canaan Road.

Right: Green River No.3 (Boniface), Madawaska Co. (standing).

Wane Edge

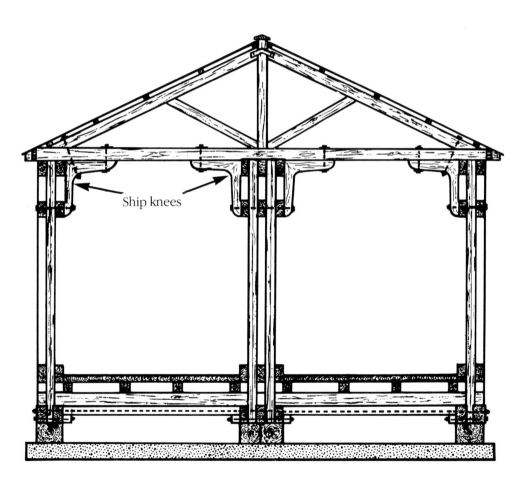

Sackville Bridge

In 1941 a sawmill at Norton, Kings Co., was given the following order for lumber to be used in bridge construction, illustrating the stringent requirements demanded by the province:

> We would like to have 10,000 feet, at least, of 2 × 6 and wider in random lengths, black spruce. This material to be sawed to true even widths and thickness; to be straight grained, free from large and loose knots, wane edges, through or round shakes, large or through season cracks, decay, worm holes or any other defects impairing its strength or durability. This lumber to be cut within the year. [see diagram of wane edge]

Ship knees were used to brace the joints of the upper chords and the side stringers. They were made from the large roots of spruce or elm. The root end had to be a full two feet with a face of seven to eight inches and the stump end between two and two and a half feet. These ship knees were a direct throwback to the province's heritage of shipbuilding.

Left: Sackville Bridge, Westmorland Co. (not standing): this drawing is based on an original, dated 1857, belonging to the Department of Transportation. We are quite sure the bridge was built soon after that date but were unable to determine if it was completely covered. Note the double lanes and the "ship knees" in the upper corners. (Based upon an original drawing by Alex L. Light, C.E., 1857. Property of N.B. Dept. of Transportation).

Tenders for Salmon River Bridge, Kings County

No.	Name	Amount	Deposit
1.	W.E. Fawcett,	$3,800.00	order
2.	C.J.B. Simmons	4,473.00	202.25
3.	A.E. Smye	4,657.00	233.00
4.	McLaggen & Boone	4,698.00	234.90
5.	Mariner M. Tingley	4,698.00	nil
6.	R.A. Logan	4,725.00	236.00
7.	Todd C. Brewer	4,950.00	250.00
8.	Joseph Goulette and John Goulette	5,000.00	250.00
9.	D.C. Burpee	5,274.00	262.35

Opened June 11th, 1907,
by T.B. Winslow & P. Hughes

BRIDGE NOTICE

SEALED TENDERS MARKED

"Tender for Salmon River Bridge,"

will be received at the Department of Public Works, Fredericton, until

MONDAY,

10th day of June, 1907, at noon,

For rebuilding Salmon River Bridge, on Smith Creek Road, Parish of Sussex, Kings Co., N. B., according to Plans and Specification to be seen at the Public Works Department, Fredericton, N. B., at the office of Hon. Wm. Pugsley, St. John, N. B., at the office of Ora P. King, M. P. P., Sussex, Kings Co., N. B. and at the store of Geo. G. Scovil, M. P. P., Belleisle Creek, Kings Co., N. B.

Each tender must be accompanied by a certified Bank Cheque or Cash, for an amount equal to five per cent of the tender, which will be forfeited if the party tendering declines to enter into contract when called upon. Should the tender be not accepted the deposit will be returned. Two good sureties must be named in each tender. Not obliged to accept lowest or any tender.

C. H. LaBILLOIS,
Chief Commissioner

Department Public Works,
Fredericton, May 16th, 1907

PANB

Right: Kennebecasis River No.8 (Salmon River or Salmon Bridge), Kings Co. (standing): this bridge has just been given a new lease on life. The local Covered Bridge Society fought to prevent its demolition and the bridge now has a lovely picnic area nearby. Fill from the excavation of the new concrete bridge was used to landscape the covered bridge.

Below: Florenceville Bridge, Carleton Co. (standing): in this old photograph, the Florenceville Bridge has four steel spans, one covered span and one small king truss in the foreground. The king truss span was later replaced with the present steel span. The bridge was officially opened on June 1, 1886. But the existing wood section was not covered until after extensive repairs in 1910. The bridge has quite a history as revealed on the plaque unveiled on June 4, 1988. The plaque reads as follows: "This bridge has endured fire and ice; witnessed birth and death; linked east and west; friends and community for over 100 years." In 1886 the body of John Lovely was found below the bridge. The second death occurred in 1915. The body of Fred Green was found in the St. John River. Clothing and traces of blood were found on the bridge.

Idle hands are the devil's tools, or what goes up must come down. There must be a good cliché to describe the situation at Hexham, Northumberland Co., in 1941. It seems the bridge crew at work in a local pit became slightly bored. To liven up the day someone slipped a few sticks of dynamite a little too close to an unoccupied storage shed. The bridge Superintendent and the Chief Bridge Engineer were not amused. The C.B.E. wrote to "J" Division of the R.C.M.P. and made the following offer:

> If you have any trouble in locating the culprit, and it will be of assistance to you, I will have the payment of the payroll for this work held up until the guilty party confesses putting the explosive on the shed.

The Chief Bridge Engineer did not see the humour in the destruction of public property.

On October 26th, 1937 Mr Charles Hirons, Esq., of Florenceville, Carleton Co., received the welcome news of his appointment as caretaker of lights on the Florenceville Bridge. The gentleman's remuneration for services was at a rate of $60.00 per year. "Your duties will consist in seeing that this bridge is lighted at the proper times and in general follow out the duties carried on by the previous caretaker."

PANB

Two factors, more than any others, led to the sudden end of the construction of covered bridges. True, the changing times took their toll. But it was the sudden popularity of pressurized chemically treated wood and the increased use of reinforced concrete which made the tedious task of boarding in a bridge unnecessary. The treated beams could stand the torment of New Brunswick's weather without a roof to fend the moisture off. Reinforced concrete was virtually impervious to the elements. The last covered bridge to be constructed in the province, by the government, was the 60-foot long Shikatehawk River No.2 (Lockhart Mill) in Kent Parish of Carleton Co. in 1954. That bridge has since been destroyed. There have been a few bridges relocated since then but no new constructions.

The most notable of these recent relocations is that of the bridge at the entrance to the game farm at Magnetic Hill. This bridge was formerly the Coverdale River #7 (Parkingdale or Tom Demille) and was moved to Moncton under the expert supervision of a bridge builder from "away back," Lower Coverdale's Austin Renton. Mr Renton tells with great pride how some of the tools used in the construction had to be borrowed or even remade to the old specifications, as in some situations modern equipment just couldn't do the job as well. If you visit this bridge, note the wooden hinges of the window. This was one of Mr Renton's finishing touches.

Bishop

Left: Parkingdale: Coverdale River No.7 (Parkingdale or Tom Demille), Albert Co. (not standing): this bridge was dismantled and then relocated at the Magnetic Hill Game Farm in Moncton. The Parkingdale bridge was built by A.E. Smye of Albert Co., while the Magnetic Hill reconstruction was supervised by Austin Renton of Lower Coverdale.

Below left: Magnetic Hill, Westmorland Co. (standing): this bridge was built in 1915 on the Coverdale River and was relocated to the Magnetic Hill Game Farm. The bridge was known as the Parkingdale or Tom Demille Bridge, named after a local school teacher. Its relocation and reconstruction was completed in 1982 under the expert supervision of Austin Renton of Lower Coverdale. Mr Renton was an employee of the Bridge Department and was responsible for the upkeep of many of the Albert and Westmorland covered bridges.

PANB

Above: Bay du Vin Bridge, Northumberland Co. (not standing): at the time of its construction there were few machines capable of moving large amounts of fill. It was much less expensive to build an approach of wood and the crib work on this bridge does not appear to be overflowing with rock, at least in the upper levels. Note the small "king truss" in the foreground of the approachway.

PANB

Sometimes it seems curious to find a 150-200 foot bridge spanning a gulch with a tiny creek at the bottom. The creek may contain relatively small amounts of water, even during the spring run-off. This is less of a mystery when the amount of landfill needed to stuff the gully is considered. In the "heyday" of bridge building, the machinery to move such large amounts of material was not available. It was cheaper to extend the length of the bridge.

The builders of the early bridges were well aware of the destructive force of the spring freshet and constructed the spans accordingly. Frequently, those travelling the back roads of the province will find a bridge perched high over the surrounding fields. The height of these abutments allowed the swollen river to flow around the ends of the bridge rather than have the bridge act as an obstacle. This usually worked; however, in the case of the William Mitton bridge, spring water carried it from its original site in Kent Co. to its present location in Albert Co.. Little wonder it became known as "The Travelling Bridge."

Left: The McBride Bridge, Carleton Co. (not standing): there must have been a high bank on the far side of the river to require the very high abutment shown in the foreground. There would be little fear of damage from the spring run-off at this bridge. The woodwork under the bridge was stone-filled but that of the approach was not. The tidy white fence was for the greater safety of night travellers.

The head of the Bridge Department was the Minister, appointed by the Premier and elected by the people. The Minister would appoint a Deputy Minister. Next in line of authority and probably the key-stone of the whole department was the Chief Bridge Engineer. This individual carried on the day-to-day business of the Department. In the decade 1920-30, expenditures up to $1,000 could be approved at the Chief Engineer's discretion. He would be familiar with the location and type of every bridge in the province, although it was the Bridge Supervisor who submitted the expenses of construction and repairs for approval. Because of their heavy workloads and the poor state of transportation throughout the province, the Chief Bridge Engineer and the Bridge Supervisor rarely saw each other.

The Bridge Supervisor was on the front line of community requests and complaints. Almost always he was someone from the local area who had previous experience on the bridge crews and had gained the confidence of the Chief Bridge Engineer. Occasionally the local Bridge Supervisor was more concerned with the welfare of his neighbours than the rigorous bookkeeping of the provincial government. In more than one instance a "down home" boy, as Supervisor, would deliberately underestimate the cost of a repair job to ensure the Department's approval for the expenditure of funds. As the work progressed the Supervisor would submit cost overruns to pay for additional labour costs, thus enhancing the local economy.

The Bridge Supervisor had a variety of duties: inspection of bridges, maintenance, construction, etc. One of his more colourful tasks was described in the Highways Act (Section 50, subsection 1):

Above: William Mitton, Albert Co. (standing): this bridge earned the nickname "the travelling bridge." However, it is not the only "travelling" bridge in the province, since several have been relocated and have therefore moved from their original position—yet not in the same manner as the William Mitton. In 1942, during particularly high spring water, the bridge was swept from Kent Co. across the line into Albert Co., where it is found today.

Every supervisor shall, as early in the winter as possible, cause the flooring of all covered bridges in his division to be covered with snow so that the same may be easily passable during the winter by sleighs and sleds.

There was a rather heated discussion between two supervisors who had the occasion to share a covered bridge. Each maintained it was the responsibility of the other to snow the bridge. The Chief Bridge Engineer had to intervene finally and again referred to the same passage in the Highways Act which states: "When any such bridge connects two highway divisions, the supervisor of each division shall cause one half of the said bridge to be covered."

So stated the law in 1941!

A lumbering outfit by the name of Reid Brothers of Gagetown received a stern warning from the Bridge Department in the summer of 1946. It seems they had been unloading logs over the side of the approach to the Starkey Bridge. There was not enough water to float the logs away and they had been piled to a height greater than the posts of the bridge itself. Fearing a sudden rise in water level would mean damage to the bridge the Reid Brothers were warned they would be held responsible for any and all damages to the structure done by their logs.

On another occasion a man caused damage to the Shediac River (Mouth) Bridge, Westmorland Co., and did not act with reasonable speed to reimburse the province for the cost of repairs. The Bridge Department threatened to place a claim on file with the Motor Vehicle Branch with instructions to withhold the issuing of the man's driving license until the account was paid in full.

A Newcastle Supervisor of Bridges got himself in hot water when he examined the damage done to the Doaktown bridge by a passing farmer. The Supervisor decided the extent of the damage was small and charged the citizen $10.00 for repairs. The Chief Bridge Engineer was not at all pleased and sent a reprimand to the Supervisor also stating that he would take the matter up with the Minister. You can be assured it was not the last that Supervisor heard of the incident.

Below: Long Creek No.1 (Starkey), Queens Co. (standing): this old photograph shows a remarkable approachway to the Starkey Bridge. Built in 1939, this structure clearly did not anticipate the demands of future traffic. The road to the entrance of the bridge has since been upgraded to present-day standards.

STARKEY (LONG'S CREEK)

It was the policy of the Bridge Department to employ local farmers whenever possible to deliver stone to the site of the work, at a rate of so much per yard. These farmers would employ members of their families or their neighbours to assist them in loading and unloading the stone. Early in the 1940s the rate of payment was $1.50 per day for horse and rig, and 30 cents per hour for each additional labourer hired.

Frequently, work was initiated on a bridge as the result of pressure from the local Committee. They represented the "grass roots" of the political system and were able to perceive the needs of the community by direct observation. For example, the following letter was sent to Fredericton requesting action. (The letter is printed unaltered.)

Waugh, N.B.
Dec. 26th, 1936

A.A. Dysart,
Minister of Public Works,
Fredericton, N.B.

Dear Mr Dysart;

As members of the Liberal Committee of Inkerman and Waugh kindly demand you to make the necessary efforts to grant the money for the repairing of Paulin's bridge at Waugh which is badly demalish since last summer.

All the lumber required, is on the spot waiting the consent of the minister of the Public Works. If that job was perform during the winter time it would accomodate the people for the spring work and also it would give some of the poor citizens work, which have large families to support, specialy for the winter months. However it is expected that a step toward the right direction will be taken to get that bridge repair before the coming spring.

Signed by the Liberal Committee;

Truly Yours,
Leo M. Landry
Alfred M. Landry
F. Landry
Patrich Godin

The Bridge Department was sometimes requested to build bridges or to do repairs on bridges on remote roads used by lumber companies. The scarcity of men and materials and the high demand for repairs to public bridges made it impossible to fulfill these requests. The Point Wolfe Bridge in Albert Co. was built in response to demands from lumbering company owners; however, a small community had grown up around the mill at Point Wolfe, thereby justifying the spending of public funds. This is one of the very few painted covered bridges in the province. (Quebec has been in the habit of painting most of its bridges but New Brunswick seems to prefer the stately grey of weathered boards.) After the formation of Fundy National Park the maintenance of the Point Wolfe Bridge became the responsibility of the Federal Government. The name Point Wolfe was chosen because someone thought the rock formation at the end of the point resembled the victorious general of the battle for the Plains of Abraham.

Left: Graham Creek (Tom Graham), Kent Co. (standing).

Point Wolfe, Albert Co. (standing): this bridge was rebuilt after falling down in 1908. A contract to rebuild at a cost of $1,456.00 was signed in 1909; however, the deal fell through. A second contract was then granted to A.E. Smye of Albert Co. dated February 1, 1910. This bridge is under the care of the National Parks of Canada. It is the only covered bridge standing which is completely painted. Most of the wooden bridges have been allowed to age naturally to their stately grey.

Bridge boards have frequently been the targets of vandals and thieves. Even today there are many recreation rooms and camp bars built of weather-aged bridge lumber. Many of the province's bridges sport new boards on their sides which take a few years to grey. To prevent this kind of nuisance at the Maxwell Crossing Bridge in the parish of Saint David in Charlotte Co., the Bridge Department instructed the Bridge Supervisor to board up the inside of the bridge for a distance of four or five feet with one inch boards. These were to be nailed on the inside of the boarding along the bridge. This would prevent the kicking off of the vertical boards on the outside.

While it seems that everyone these days feels overworked and underpaid, this is not a new phenomenon. In 1941, the caretaker of the Narrows Bridge in Queens Co. wrote a request to the Chief Bridge Engineer expressing a concern about having to open the bridge to river traffic at nights and on Sundays. The response was to point out the legal obligation. "The draw, of course, will have to be opened at any time navigation demands it, as according to Navigation Law shipping must not be held up by the bridges."

Above: The Narrows Bridge, Queens Co. (not standing): a caretaker was on duty to open the bridge for navigation when the need arose. After complaining of his extra duties, one such caretaker was given a small raise in pay to compensate him. This tremendous bridge was destroyed during the infamous "Ground Hog Day Gale" in 1976.

Right: Dennis Stream No.3 (Maxwell Crossing), Charlotte Co. (standing).

42

Above: Iroquois River No.4, Madawaska Co. (standing).

Right: Milkish Inlet No.1 (Bayswater), Kings Co. (standing): permission had to be granted from Ottawa before work could be done on this 1920 bridge. Any structure over waters that may be used by large boats must meet the requirements of the Federal Navigable Waters Protection Act

The Navigable Waters Protection Act (Chapter 115, Revised Statutes of Canada, 1906) meant the province had to seek permission any time it wished to bridge a body of water that was passable by shipping. The Milkish Inlet No.1 (Bayswater) bridge of Kings Co., required Federal approval before it was constructed in 1920.

> The Committee of the Privy Council have before them a Report, dated 10th September, 1919, a request for approval of ... a fixed bridge proposed to be built over Milkish Creek, in the Parish of Westfield, Kings Co., New Brunswick, to replace the present draw bridge.

The Minister states that the District Engineer of the Department of Public Works at St. John has recommended that the application be approved, provided that the clearance of the new bridge be 6'6" greater than the draw span of the old bridge, that is, that the present top of cap at the upstream westerly corner of the present draw span.

The Federal Minister accepted that the new bridge would be satisfactory if the provincial government would agree, if called upon to do so in the future, to insert a draw span in the interest of navigation.

The employees of the Bridge Department had to be true "Jack's of all trades" who donned the hats of engineers, accountants, carpenters, public relations experts and so on. Perhaps the most unusual demand asked of the Department came in 1918. A woman wrote complaining of the way her husband had been treating her. Her spouse was a Bridge Supervisor in Northumberland Co.. The distraught wife was demanding that half of her husband's salary be paid to her and if that were not possible, that her husband be fired. The response from the Department was sympathetic but reminded the wife that this was a matter for the courts to decide.

As for your request, as an alternative to have him dismissed from service as a punishment for his conduct towards you, I can only say that it is not my place to act as judge in such a matter, as the conduct of an officer towards his family has nothing to do whatever with his efficiency in the discharge of the duties of his office.

This reply was from P.J. Veniot, Minister of Public Works.

Left: Digdeguash River No.4 (McCann), Charlotte Co. (standing).

Right: Coles Island West Bridge, Queens Co. (not standing): there is a door in the middle of this bridge which allowed Bridge Department personnel to examine the structure. Judging from the amount of timber in the river, the door was probably also useful to lumbermen when freeing logs caught up on the abutments. Note the logs piled in the foreground waiting to be floated. On the opposite side of the river is a large, overturned scow.

Right: Kouchibouguacis No.5 (Cameron Mill), Kent Co. (standing).

Below: Magaguadavic River No.7 (Flume Ridge), Charlotte Co. (standing).

Of 73 covered bridges in the Province today, only 5 are of the Burr Truss design (see illustration, p.11). The remainder of the structures are Howe Trusses.

In 1941 the going rate for expropriated land was $200.00 an acre.

Left: Canal Bridge, Charlotte Co. (standing).

Right: Digdeguash River No.2 (Stillwater), Charlotte Co. (standing).

PANB

The youngest bridge, Quisibis River No.2, Madawaska Co., was built in 1952. (Relocations are not new bridges, e.g. Magnetic Hill.)

The oldest bridges are Nelson Hollow, Northumberland Co. (renovated in 1899) or Keswick River No.7, Burnside Hayne, York Co. (1899).

Above: North Becaguimec River No.4 (Ellis), Carleton Co. (standing).

Right: Baker Brook No.2 (Morneault Settlement), Madawaska Co. (standing): very few of the standing bridges have the old-fashioned shingle roof. Most, like this bridge, have had the original covering replaced with steel.

A great deal of confusion often arises over the correct names of some of New Brunswick's bridges. One bridge may be known by several titles or, even worse, several bridges may share the same name. For instance, The Salmon Bridge is or was a name found on various rivers throughout the province. A letter from the Albert Manufacturing Company to A.R. Wetmore of the Bridge Department, dated January 16, 1901, illustrates the problem:

> Brookton Bridge on Brookton road is correct, and if Mr Haines reports the bridge near Harris McLatchey Steeves as Bull Creek Bridge, I have no doubt this is the correct name, but I did not know it when referring to it in previous communications.

In Albert Co., Bamford Colpits operated a saw mill which supplied lumber for several projects. It is not surprising therefore to find the Bamford Colpits Bridge nearby.

The Ryan Bridge once stood in York Co. and gained an interesting nickname—The Bridge To Nowhere. P.G. Ryan was a Commissioner of Bridges at the turn of the century and he had predicted a rise in population on the far side of the Nashwaak river. His prediction was a miss and nothing ever developed although some lumber was hauled over the bridge. The approaches to the structure eventually returned to their natural state, leaving the bridge in the middle of nowhere.

W.M. Starkey of Cody's, Queens Co., wrote to the Bridge Department concerning repairs to a local bridge. In his opinion, stone fill needed for the job could be obtained in considerable quantities about a mile from the bridge.

> In Mr Starkey's opinion [the stone] could be hauled cheaper on sleds in the winter. Mr Starkey also states that he has

BRIDGE NOTICE.

SEALED TENDERS, MARKED

"Tender for Bull Creek Bridge,"

will be received at the Department of Public Works, Fredericton, until

MONDAY,

11th day of February, 1901, at noon,

For rebuilding Bull Creek Bridge, Salem, Albert Co., N. B., according to Plan and Specification to be seen at the Public Works Department, at Mr. Ryan's, M. P. P., Coverdale, Albert Co., and at the office of Mr. C. J. Osman, M. P. P., Hillsborough, Albert Co.

Each tender must be accompanied by a certified Bank Cheque or Cash, for an amount equal to five per cent. of the tender (would prefer not receiving P. O. Orders) which will be forfeited if the party tendering declines to enter into contract when called upon. Should the tender be not accepted the deposit will be returned. Two good sureties must be named in each tender. Not obliged to accept lowest or any tender.

C. H. LaBILLOIS,
Chief Commissioner.

Department Public Works,
Fredericton, January 24th, 1901

PANB

a quantity of poplar trees that he would sell to put in the bottom of the tray on which to pile the stone to keep it from settling into the mud.

We might well be inspired by the civic-minded Mr Starkey. But who was better to care for the structure known as the Starkey Bridge, Queens Co.?

After the Second World War, a government employee by the name of Dodge decided to standardize the bridge names. He devised a plan whereby the bridges were to be designated in the order of their sequence from the mouth of the river or stream. In this way, the "Picadilly" or "Urney" became "Trout Creek No.4" and "Moores Mill Bridge" became "Trout Creek No.5." The bridges on the major rivers, the Saint John or the Miramichi, did not receive such

designations. The system did have its attraction for those craving order and clarity but how could "Hartley Steeves-Dan Cupid" ever be replaced by "Weldon Creek No. 5"?

Left: Bull Creek (Harris Steeves), Albert Co. (standing): this bridge spans Bull Creek in Albert Co. It is one of a pair of bridges being very near the Hartley Steeves-Dan Cupid Bridge. See the photograph on page 1 showing both bridges. This bridge was built by W.R. Fawcett.

Right: Coverdale River No.3 (Bamford Colpitts), Albert Co. (standing): we were very impressed by the quaint beauty of this old structure.

In 1972, a group of concerned citizens decided to do something to halt the declining condition of the Province's covered bridges. The group named itself The League for Rural Renewal and members of the League met the following requirements:

a) retirement from their life's principal vocation;

b) a keen interest in the quality of rural life in New Brunswick;

c) the ability and desire to help do something to improve it [rural life in N.B.].

The League received monies from the federal government's Department of Health and Welfare, under the New Horizons Programme, and a Biblical quotation often cited in the League's public statements seemed more than appropriate for the task they had chosen: "Remove not thy ancient landmarks which thy fathers have set." (Proverbs, 22:28)

Land was leased to the League by the owners of property adjacent to certain bridges at a cost of one dollar per year. The agreement could be cancelled at the end of the year should either party become dissatisfied. Local support for the projects was encouraged at every opportunity. It was the League's hope that the various communities would maintain the improvements once they had been achieved.

There was a desire on the part of the provincial government to help the League wherever possible. The Department of Highways provided repairs to the bridges and supplied the machinery for the heavy work on the sites if necessary. The Department of Tourism provided picnic furniture. The Department of Agriculture and the Rural Development and Historical Resources administrations also provided support.

The first bridge to receive the attention of the League was the Patrick Owen (Rusagonis). This was in the fall of 1973, and the local initiative was headed by the Women's Institute with a financial grant of $3,000.00 from the New Horizons programme. Plumweseep, Kings Co., was ready for a formal opening by mid-summer of 1974. By the end of the 1974 season, six more bridges were upgraded.

The Daily Gleaner

Left: Colter 'Transplant,' York Co. (not standing): reassembling the bridge on the Keswick.

Trout Creek No.4 (Picadilly or Urney), Kings Co. (standing).

In 1972, the Colter Bridge on the Keswick River had been destroyed by arson. When it became known that at the same time several bridges were being dismantled at the junction of the Gaspereau and the Salmon Rivers, the concept of a transplant appealed to the League for Rural Renewal. The Canadian Armed Forces authorities at Base Gagetown were eager for some practical experience for their Corps of Engineers (along with a visiting detachment of U.S. Army engineers); they therefore dismantled one of the Gaspereau River bridges and reassembled it on the Keswick. The Colter family, after which the burnt bridge had been named, supplied the lumber required to replace the aged abutments. Twenty-five thousand feet of timber were moved from the Miramichi to Tracy to be chemically treated, then on to the construction site. The Department of Transportation transported the material and funded the chemical treatment.

The task of replacing the old abutments was shared by the Department of Transportation, C.F.B. Gagetown, and volunteers. By the late summer of 1976 the bridge was reassembled and in October of the same year some three hundred people gathered to celebrate the official opening of the bridge. The excitement and charm of the event was described in the second issue of the booklet "Behind the Bushes," a report of the activities of The League for Rural Renewal:

> After introductions, remarks by a member of the League, the commander of the Base and officials of the Department of Transportation, all three signed documents for officially turning back to the Department of Transportation the finished bridge with whose segments all had been playing with for so long. The ribbon was formally cut by the young woman who originated the petition, supported by the soldier of the Canadian military engineers whose work had received special commendation. Facing the entrance of the bridge was a team of handsome horses with the brass of their harness gleaming in the sun, hitched to a long flat-topped dray on which had been set bales of hay for seats. All seats were crowded with cheering children from the community of Keswick and the surrounding area. Headed by the bagpipes the team with its load was driven through the bridge followed under their own power, by half a dozen vintage motor cars almost as ancient as the bridge itself, and all loaded with guests in holiday mood. When all was over the army invited everybody to the marquee tent where it acted as host with refreshments.

The wonderful story of the Colter Transplant had one final dramatic, and tragic, twist. The night before Hallowe'en 1977, one year after the reconstruction ceremony, the bridge was again burned into the water. In seconds it was engulfed in flames and in minutes there was nothing to be saved.

Two Ontario men were convicted of the crime and were sentenced to 2½ years imprisonment. But they had done their dirty work and the Colter Bridge has not been replaced again.

The League for Rural Renewal has faded, due in no small part to the death of several key members. Anyone in New Brunswick who treasures its heritage is greatly in debt to the excellent individuals who founded the League. The plight of the province's covered bridges would be much worse than it is without their timely efforts.

The Daily Gleaner

Far left: Colter 'Transplant,' York Co. (not standing): the finishing touches are been put to the reassembled bridge.

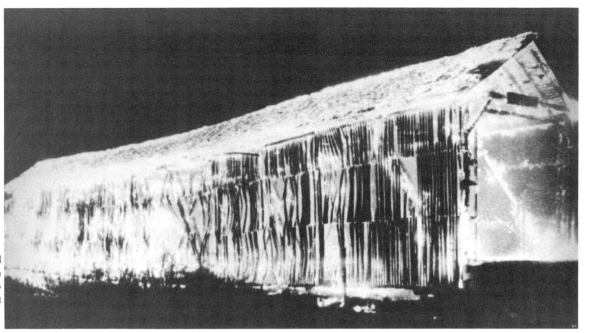

Above: Colter 'Transplant,' York Co. (not standing): the fire was started by arsonists and burned so quickly that nothing could be done to save the bridge. This remarkable photograph was taken by Louella Billings, staff photographer for *The Daily Gleaner.*

Left: Colter 'Transplant,' York Co. (not standing): the remains of a very special bridge.

Red Bank 1, Northumberland Co. (not standing): this was the Red Bank Bridge constructed in 1905 across the Northwest Branch of the Miramichi River. At 979 feet it was one of the longest covered bridges built in the province. The bridge was burned on April 13, 1954.

BRIDGE NOTICE.

SEALED TENDERS MARKED

"Tender for Red Bank Bridge,"

will be received at the Department of Public Works, Fredericton, until

MONDAY,

13th day of March, 1905, at noon,

For Rebuilding Red Bank Bridge, over N. W. Miramichi River, Parish of North Esk, Northumberland Co., according to Plan and Specification to be seen at the Public Works Department, Fredericton, and at the office of Hon. L. J. Tweedie, Premier, Chatham, N. B.

Each tender must be accompanied by a certified Bank Cheque or Cash, for an amount equal to five per cent of the tender, which will be forfeited if the party tendering declines to enter into contract when called upon. Should the tender be not accepted the deposit will be returned. Two good sureties must be named in each tender Not obliged to accept lowest or any tender.

Department Public Works,
Fredericton, February 22nd, 1905

C. H. LaBILLOIS,
Chief Commissioner.

PANB

The Red Bank Bridge

Whenever someone mentions covered bridges there is a tendency for New Brunswickers to recall the bridges near which they spent their childhoods. "I grew up just down the road from that bridge" was a phrase we heard over and over again. There is not a person raised in rural New Brunswick who cannot place memories near one of the old structures. The authors are among those folks. We grew up about a mile from the old Red Bank Bridge. With seven Howe truss spans and a length of 979 feet, it was an impressive sight. If it were standing today, only the Hartland bridge would be longer.

The original bridge was constructed at the request of the local residents in 1879. This was replaced in 1905 with a second bridge, the Red Bank covered bridge, which stood until it was burned on April 13, 1954. Its replacement was a creosoted Howe Truss bridge which was also burned in 1970. The present bridge is made of reinforced concrete.

Saint Thomas Parish, Red Bank

Left: Red Bank 4, Northumberland Co. (not standing): there are a few more grave markers in the cemetery at Red Bank today than there were in this old photograph. The old Red Bank Covered Bridge holds back the timber on the Main North West Miramichi. The birthplace of well-known Miramichi storyteller, Garfield Matchett, stands at the far end of the bridge.

Right: Red Bank 3, Northumberland Co. (not standing): Sunday afternoon excitement on the North West Miramichi under the old covered bridge at Red Bank.

Below: This is what remained of the Red Bank Bridge the day following the fire.

Mrs M. Tozer

E.F. Gillis

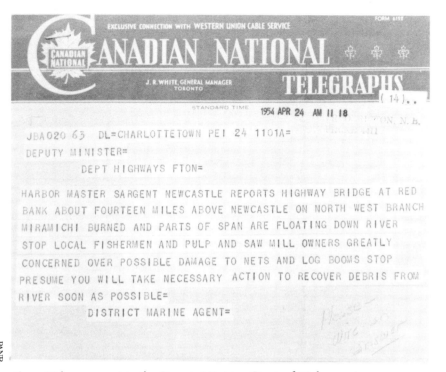

Above: Telegram sent to the Deputy Minister, Dept. of Highways, in Fredericton, announces the destruction of the Red Bank Bridge, on April 24, 1954:

Harbour Master Sargeant Newcastle reports highway bridge at Red Bank about fourteen miles above Newcastle on North West Branch Miramichi burned and parts of span are floating down river STOP local fishermen and pulp and saw mill owners greatly concerned over possible damage to nets and log booms STOP presume you will take necessary action to recover debris from river as soon as possible.

District Marine Agent

Bloomfield Bridge

There is something special about growing up on the banks of a river. The seasonal variations seem more noticeable when reflected in the water's surface. Summer on the river is entirely special; long days are spent swimming at the "hole" with the gang. The kaleidoscope of autumn is followed by the frozen grip of winter when kids play hockey on cold Saturday mornings. However, the most dramatic of all seasons near the river is spring. The slow, predictable waterway annually swells to become a formidable torrent during the season of the spring freshet.

A Kings County woman, Connie Neales, recalled the days of her childhood when, as a student at the Bloomfield School, she was forced to contend with the swollen Kennebecasis during the floods. The Bloomfield covered bridge was fairly high at one end but opened to a large, low-lying marsh at the other. The marsh would submerge for days as the melt-water rushed seaward.

Several children who attended the little school lived on the opposite side of the river. In the years when the water was especially high, special arrangements were made to transport the students. There was a man who lived on the far side of the river and owned a sturdy boat. The school officials kept a bell on a box at the distant end of the old covered bridge. When the children arrived on the bridge they would ring the bell and the man would bring his boat out to get them. The other kids were always envious as students from across the river were dismissed half an hour early.

BRIDGE NOTICE

SEALED TENDERS, MARKED

Tender for Bloomfield Creek Bridge

will be received at the Department of Public Works, Fredericton, until

WEDNESDAY

26th DAY OF SEPTEMBER, 1917, AT 5 O'CLOCK, P.M.

For Rebuilding Bloomfield Creek Bridge, Parish of Norton, King's County, N.B., according to Plans and Specifications to be seen at the Public Works Department, Fredericton, N.B., at the Provincial Government Rooms, St. John, N.B., and at the store of W. A. Saunders & Sons, Bloomfield, King's County, N.B.

Each tender must be accompanied by a CERTIFIED Bank Cheque or Cash for an amount equal to five per cent. of the tender, which will be forfeited if the party tendering declines to enter into contract when called upon. Such Certified Bank Cheque or Cash will be returned to the parties whose tenders are not accepted, but with the party to whom the contract is awarded, it shall be retained until the final completion of the contract and its acceptance by the Department. Not obliged to accept lowest or any tender.

Department of Public Works,
Fredericton, N.B., Sept. 5th, 1917

P. J. VENIOT
MINISTER OF PUBLIC WORKS

PANB

Right: Bloomfield Creek, Kings Co. (standing).

Below: From Mill Brook No.1 (Nelson Hollow), Northumberland Co. (standing): this information appears on the inside of the Nelson Hollow Bridge. If its claim to be built about 1870 is correct, this is the oldest confirmed standing covered bridge in New Brunswick. The Nelson Hollow is one of two standing bridges which have the "hip" or "cottage" roof. The bridge is closed to public traffic. If it were not for the concern of the Doaktown Historical Society it is doubtful whether this bridge would still exist.

Above: This *No Smoking* sign was a clear warning, but bridges sometimes carried placards for paid advertising.

NELSON HOLLOW
BRIDGE

Built Approx. 1870
Renovated Completely 1899

Restored in 1977
through the efforts of

Doaktown Historical Society

The Hartland Bridge

The province of New Brunswick has a great deal to be proud of. It boasts scenery second to none, with rivers broad and deep. Its coastline is lengthy and unspoiled. But there is one special attraction that every good New Brunswicker is quick to point out—we have the longest covered bridge in the world.

The Hartland Bridge was built in the years 1898-1899 by a privately financed organization known as the Hartland Toll Bridge Company. On March 8th, 1907, the New Brunswick Legislature passed "An Act to abolish tolls on Hartland Bridge."

Whereas, pursuant to the provisions, of the Act 62 Victoria Chapter 5, a bridge was erected by the Hartland Bridge Company across the Saint John River, at Hartland, in the County of Carleton;

And, whereas, in order to enable the Company to construct such bridge, the Lieutenant Governor in Council did, persuant to the authority contained in said Act, guarantee the Company's bonds, and the said bridge has since been maintained as a toll bridge;

And, whereas, the said bridge affords much needed accommodation to a large number of people, and it is considered desirable in the public interest that such bridge should be made free;

And whereas, the shareholders of the said Company paid in upon their stock on or about the twenty-fourth day of April, A.D., 1899, the sum of five hundred dollars, and have received no interest thereon:

Be it therefore enacted by the Lieutenant Governor and Legislative Assembly, as follows:—

The Lieutenant Governor in Council is hereby authorized to acquire the stock of the said Company for the amount paid in upon the same by the shareholders of the Company, and interest thereon, at the rate of five per centum per annum, from the twenty-fourth day April, A.D., 1899, not exceeding in the whole for principal and interest, the sum of seven hundred dollars, and thereupon the Receiver General shall pay the interest upon said bonds out of current revenues and shall pay the principal thereof at maturity, and the said bridge shall thereupon be and become of the public bridges off the Province, and shall be maintained by the Department of Public Works, the same as other public bridges.

The original bridge structure consisted of six piers and two abutments of cribwork construction. For a detailed description of

Opposite: Hartland Bridge, Carleton Co. (standing): this turn-of-the-century photograph shows the world's longest covered bridge before it was covered. Note the lumber accumulated at the point of each abutment.

Below: Hartland Bridge, Carleton Co. (standing): this photograph is entitled "Covered Bridge, Hartland, N.B., 19 July 1932." Note the different level to the roof of the first two spans when compared to the other five. This is a reminder of the 1920 spring freshet when the ice damaged the first two piers in the foreground. When the bridge was repaired the slight variation in the height of the roof marked the occasion.

PAC

the bridge (even if it gets a little technical) who better to quote than the Chief Bridge Engineer of the Department of Public Works. In 1950, replying to a request for information, C.A. MacVey wrote:

[The piers] were provided at the upstream end with ice guards, or cut water noses, 45 degrees angle, to take care of the tremendous ice push or run in the river every spring. The noses of the old piers were sheathed with 4 inch hardwood. This sheathing extended around the sides of the piers a distance of about 20 feet. These piers and abutments did service until 1920, when they were replaced with concrete piers and abutments. These also being designed with cut water noses on the upstream ends of the piers. This work was done by contract—Powers Construction Company being the contractors. The inspector on the work was R.C. Fletcher. ... The Powers Construction Company went south to Miami some years after this contract was completed, and was busily engaged for many years in the construction of levees on the Mississippi River.

The original spans were open Howe trusses, but were later covered in; additional bracing being added to take care of the wind load, which naturally increased by the covering in of the spans. These spans were also replaced in 1920 under the Powers contract. There are 7 Howe truss spans about 177 feet in length—3 play chords. The clear width of roadway on the spans being 18 feet. Chord material is of B.C. douglas fir. The web members and most of the floor beams are of New Brunswick black spruce. The total length of the bridge is 1,282 feet from end to end of spans.

In 1944, the Bridge Department rebuilt the approach on the village end of the bridge. The original approach consisted of stone filled cribwork. This was dismantled and a new approach was built consisting of reinforced concrete trestle bents and slab spans.

In the spring of 1919, James Neals of Kings Co. was in Hartland to attend a wedding. He was met at the train station by a driver, as had been arranged, and proceeded to cross the Hartland Covered Bridge. When they neared the far end of the bridge, they noticed a crowd of people gathered on the approachway. The two men stopped their carriage on the bridge and peered upstream to see what the fuss was all about, in time to see the ice gather dangerously at the piers. Without further hesitation, they leaped into their vehicle, whipped up the horse, and cleared the bridge as the ice swept away the last two piers on the uphill side.

Right: Hartland Bridge, Carleton Co. (standing): at 1282 feet from end-to-end, the Hartland is the longest covered bridge in the world. The original bridge was constructed in the years 1898-99 by the privately owned Hartland Toll Bridge Company. In 1920, however, most of the bridge was replaced. The wooden piers and abutments were replaced with reinforced concrete. The original spans were open Howe Trusses and were covered in. In 1944 the Bridge Department rebuilt the approach at the Village end.

The building of this bridge was not without controversy. In William C. Carr's *High and Dry* (1938) he wrote:

'The Government contract called for the [Hartland] bridge we were constructing across the St. John River to be a covered bridge. As the work progressed the good folk got together and thought the bridge should not be covered. The reason being that they thought it would provide

a dark place where the boys and girls of the town might find opportunity to do things which they were not supposed to do until married. Len _____ and I went to hear a Baptist minister preach on the subject one Sunday evening. The preacher condemned the idea of covering the bridge in no uncertain terms. He said that to cover it would turn it into a potential ram pasture. Public opinion was so roused that a petition was circulated; it requested the Government to have the plans changed, and in the petition they gave as their reason "that to cover the bridge would seriously jeopardize the morals of the young people of Hartland."

The bridge was covered in spite of the petition and I saw a letter written to the contractors in reference to it, in which a member of the Government had said: "If the morals of the young people are so badly bent that it only requires a covered bridge to break them completely, there is little we, as the Government, can do about the matter."'

Above: Barkers Point Bridge, York Co. (not standing): this was an unusual bridge, located at Barkers Point, near Fredericton. Note the numerous windows and the sidewalk. The roof has two levels. The man in the foreground is unidentified.

Left: Black River Bridge, Northumberland Co. (not standing): the sign at the end of the bridge reads, "$20.00 fine for driving faster than a walk on this bridge." This was an especially tidy little bridge with its painted portals and eaves. Note the white fence posts with the carefully painted tops. Someone took a great deal of pride in the appearance of this old structure

Eel River No.3 (Benton), York Co. (standing).

Appendix A
Standing Covered Bridges by County

These figures are based on information from the New Brunswick Department Of Transportation, revised in 1981. The figure given represents the total length of the bridge in question.

The trusses are Howe design unless otherwise indicated. 'Burr' designates an Arched-Burr or Strutted-Burr truss design.

Name	Parish	Length	Year Built	Truss
Albert Co. (10 bridges)				
Bull Creek (Harris Steeves)	Hillsborough	90'	1927	
Coverdale River No.3 (Bamford Colpitts)	Coverdale	104'10"		Burr
Crooked Creek No.3	Hopewell	98'2"		
Lower Forty Five No.1	Alma	101'		
William Mitton	Coverdale	82'		Burr
Point Wolfe	Alma	95'	1910	
Saw Mill Creek No.1	Hopewell	105'	1905	
Shepody River No.3 (Germantown Lake)	Harvey	63'	1908	
Turtle Creek No.4 (Peter Jonah) *64' covered; 24'2" open	Hillsborough	*85'2"		
Weldon Creek No.3 (Hartley Steeves)	Hillsborough	63'8"	1923	
Carleton County (6 bridges)				
Becaguimec River No.3 (Mangrum)	Brighton	97'8"	1909	

Province of New Brunswick

RESTIGOUCHE
(0)

MADAWASKA
(4)

GLOUCESTER
(0)

NORTHUMBERLAND
(1)

VICTORIA
(1)

CARLETON
(6)

KENT
(4)

YORK
(4)

WESTMORLAND
(7)

QUEENS
(4)

ALBERT
(10)

SUNBURY
(4)

KINGS
(17)

ST. JOHN (3)

CHARLOTTE
(8)

73 covered bridges standing

Above: Nerepis River No.3 (Bayard), Queens Co. (standing).

Florenceville Bridge *one covered span measuring 154'	Peel & Simonds	*950'	1910	
Hartland	Brighton & Wakefield	1282'	1921	
Monquart River No.3 (Keenan)	Kent	89'	1927	
North Becaguimec River No.1 (Adair)	Brighton	68'	1948	
North Becaguimec River No.4 (Ellis)	Brighton	63'	1909	

Charlotte County (8 bridges)

Canal Covered Bridge	St. George	127'6"	1917	
Dennis Stream No.3 (Maxwell Crossing)	St. Stephen	63'6"	1910	
Digdeguash River No.2 (Stillwater)	St. Patrick	94'	1901	Burr
Digdeguash River No.3 (McGuire)	St. Patrick	118'6"	1915	
Digdeguash River No.4 (McCann)	Dumbarton	89'	1938	
Digdeguash River No.6 (Dumbarton)	Dumbarton	78'6"	1928	
Little Lepreau R. No.1 (Mill Pond)	Lepreau	108'10"	1910	
Magaguadavic Riv. No.7 (Flume Ridge)	Dumbarton	63'	1905	Burr

Right: North Becaguimec River No.1 (Adair), Carleton Co. (standing).

Below: Digdeguash River No.6 (Dumbarton), Charlotte Co. (standing).

Crooked Creek No.3, Albert Co. (standing): when we were photographing this bridge, a hunter walked up to our car and seemed quite confused. We hesitated to upset anyone with a rifle in his hands but soon learned he had been lost since early morning and had followed the Crooked Creek until he discovered us some six or seven hours later.

Kent County (4 bridges)

St. Nicholas River No.1 (East Branch)	Weldford & Richibucto	79'	1925
Kouchibouguacis No.5 (Camerons Mill)	St. Louis	202'6"	1950
Graham Creek (Tom Graham)	Weldford	63'	1928
St. Nicholas Riv. No.1 (Mouth)	Weldford & Richibucto	502'	1919

Kings Co. (17 bridges)

Belleisle Creek No.2 (Marven)	Springfield	79'	1903
Bloomfield Creek	Norton	151'	1917
Kennebecasis Riv. No.8 (Salmon)	Studholm	119'6"	1907
Kennebecasis Riv. No.9 (Plumweseep)	Sussex	78'	1910
Kennebecasis Riv. No.23 (Malone)	Cardwell	64'	1910
Milkish Inlet No.1 (Bayswater)	Westfield	218'	1920
Millstream No.5 (Centreville)	Studholm	100'2"	1911
Smith Creek No.1 (Tranton)	Studholm	127'	1925
Smith Creek No.5 (Oldfield)	Studholm	97'10"	1910

Above: Back Creek No.2 (Hoyt Station), Sunbury Co. (standing).

Above: Hammond River No.2 (French Village), Kings Co. (standing): the French Village Bridge is the site of a busy camp ground in the summer months. In September and October, during the salmon season, anglers stop to look down from the bridge to see what lies in the clear waters below.

Left: St. Nicholas River No.1 (Mouth), Kent Co. (standing).

Trout Creek No.3 (Bell)	Sussex	78'	1903
Trout Creek No.4 (Picadilly, Urney)	Waterford	68'6	1905
Trout Creek No.5 (Moores Mills)	Waterford	63'8"	1923
Wards Creek No.2 (MacFarlane)	Sussex	63'6"	1909
Darlings Island	Hampton	140'5"	1915
Hammond River No.2 (French Village)	Hampton & Rothesay	187'6"	1919
Hammond River No.3 (Smithtown)	Hampton	186'9"	1912
Moosehorn	Norton	98'	

Above: Wards Creek No.2 (MacFarlane), Kings Co. (standing).

Madawaska County (4 bridges)

Baker Brook No.2 (Morneault Settlement)	Baker Brook	98'6"	1939
Green River No.3 (Boniface)	St. Basile	194'	1925
Iroquois River No.4	Madawaska	78'	1924
Quisibis River No.2	St. Anne	66'	1951

Northumberland County (1 bridge)

Nelson Hollow *Built approx. 1870, renovated in 1899	Ludlow	78'	*1899

Above: Belleisle Creek No.2 (Marvin), Kings Co. (standing).

Below: Monquart River No.3 (Keenan), Carleton Co. (standing).

Below: South Oromocto River No.2 (Mill Settlement), Sunbury Co. (standing).

Above: Keswick River No.6 (Stone Ridge), York Co. (standing).

Above: Quisibis River No.2, Madawaska Co. (standing).

Queens County (4 bridges)

Canaan River No.1 (Aaron Clark)	Brunswick	164'	1927
Gaspereau River No.2 (Burpee)	Chipman	167'9"	1913
Long Creek No.1 (Starkey)	Johnston	225'8"	1939
Nerepis River No.3 (Bayard)	Petersville	107'6"	

Saint John (3 bridges)

Vaughan Creek No.2 (Hardscrabble)	St. Martins	78'4"	1947
Tynemouth Creek	Simonds	97'2"	
Vaughan Creek No.1 (Irish River)	St. Martins	78'6"	1935

Sunbury County (4 bridges)

Back Creek No.2 (Hoyt Station)	Blissville	67'	1909
Rusagonis River No.2 (Patrick Owen)	Lincoln	236'	1909
South Oromocto R. No.2 (Mill Settlement)	Blissville	139'2"	1915
South Oromocto R. No.3 (Bell)	Blissville	126'4"	1930

Shediac River No.4 (Joshua Gallant), Westmorland Co. (standing).

Victoria County (1 bridge)

Odellach River No.2 (Tomilson Mill)	Gordon	63'	1918

Westmorland County (7 bridges)

Cocagne River No.3 (Poirier)	Moncton	145'8"	1942
Cocagne River No.5 (Budd)	Moncton	89'	1913
Memramcook River No.4 (Boudreau)	Dorchester	78'6"	1930

Right: Memramcook River No.4 (Boudreau), Westmorland Co. (standing).

Above: Trout Creek No.3 (Bell), Kings Co. (standing): the fence and picnic tables are the legacy of The League for Rural Renewal.

Right: Cocagne River No.5 (Budd), Westmorland Co. (standing).

78

Petitcodiac River No.3 (Hasty)	Salisbury	126'4"	1931	
Shediac River No.4 (Joshua Gallant)	Shediac	90'	1935	
Tantramar River No.2 (Wheaton)	Sackville	167'10"	1910	
Magnetic Hill *relocation date, originally built in 1922	Moncton	62'	*1982	

York County (4 bridges)

Eel River No.3 (Benton)	Canterbury & Woodstock	107'6"	—	
Keswick River No.6 (Stone Ridge)	Bright & Douglas	127'	1914	
Keswick River No.7 (Burnside-Haynes)	Bright & Douglas	93'	1899	Burr
Nackawic River No.5 (Nackawic Siding)	Southampton	63'		

Appendix B

The photographs included in this section, of New Brunswick bridges no longer in existence, have been selected primarily because they illustrate special features of design or construction or because a particular event or anecdote is attached to a bridge's memory. In some cases, however, we were guided by the quality of the print or by geographical location.

A more comprehensive pictorial record of non-standing bridges could undoubtedly be gathered and we hope that some day someone will attempt to gather in all the remaining precious images of this lost heritage.

Left: Notre-Dame, Kent Co. (not standing): this bridge spanned the Cocagne River.

Below: Richardson or Forks Bridge, Queens Co. (not standing): perched high above the water this old double span sports a "hip" or "cottage" roof. The old bridges were frequently built this high to allow unrestricted passage for the swollen waters of the spring freshet

Schwetz

PANB

Above: Marysville, York Co. (not standing): the sides were not boarded in on this bridge which once spanned the Nashwaak River at Marysville. Note the newly-constructed cotton mill in the background.

Left: Porter Cove Bridge after ice run, Main South West Miramichi, Northumberland Co.(not standing). Note the footbridge.

Right: Big Salmon River, Saint John Co. (not standing): this bridge stood at the mouth of Big Salmon River.

Below: Hunters Ferry, Queens Co. (not standing): a six-span bridge constructed from 1912 to 1914. Vandals burned the bridge to the water in 1975.

PANB

PANB

82

Above: Lockhart Mills, Carleton Co. (not standing), stood on the Shikatehawk River.

Left: Upper Blackville Bridge, Northumberland Co. (not standing): the sign on this bridge gives the name "Donald Bridge." Note the beautifully shaped piers.

Above: Burnt Land Brook, Boiestown, Northumberland Co., 1920 (not standing).

Right: Ryan Brook Mouth Bridge, Kings Co. (not standing): an advertisement at the entrance of the bridge read "Clothing-Oak Hall." Oak Hall was a prominent store on King Street in nearby Saint John.

Left: Ryan Bridge, Kings Co. (not standing): there was a Ryan Bridge in York Co., and a Ryan Brook Mouth Bridge, also in Kings Co., in addition to the bridge shown here. P.G. Ryan was a Commissioner of Public Works at the turn of the century.

Below: Hawkes Bridge, Kings Co. (not standing).

Above: Fernmount Bridge, Sunbury Co. (not standing), crossed the Burpee Millstream.

Right: Sharp Bridge, Kings Co. (not standing).

SHARP (Geo's) BRIDGE

Above: A view of the bridge that once stood at Plaster Rock, Victoria Co., 1910 (not standing).

Left: Lester Bridge, Kings Co. (not standing). Note the footprints in the sand. Crossing on foot did not necessitate a bridge.

LESTER BRIDGE

This photograph is entitled *Milltown Dam, Passamaquoddy Bay, N.B., 1919.*

Schwetz

Left: Upper Dorchester, Westmorland Co. (not standing): this bridge once crossed the Memramcook River and was 848 feet in length.

Below: Red Bank Bridge, Queens Co., near Chipman (not standing).

PANB

Bishop

Left: Riverview Bridge, Parkingdale, Albert Co. (not standing).

Below: Wallace Blakeny Bridge, Westmorland Co. (not standing): this structure spanned the North River.

Schwetz

Above: Titus Bridge, Kings Co. (not standing).

Left: Second Falls, Charlotte Co. (not standing): this bridge stood on the Magaguadavic River.

91

Schwetz

Above: Linton Bridge, Bonnie River, Charlotte Co. (not standing)

Right: Alma, Salmon River (Mouth) Bridge, Albert Co. (not standing): at one time this bridge had a moveable span. It opened to allow schooners' passage upstream, from the Bay of Fundy, to load lumber at a mill nearby. This bridge was dismantled in 1969. It was built by A.E. Smye.

Schwetz

Right: McConnell Bridge, Westmorland Co. (not standing): this bridge, which stood on the Cocagne River, was destroyed when hit by a truck which went out of control on an icy winter day.

Schwetz

Left: The Gill Bridge, Northumberland Co. (not standing).

GILL

PANB

93

Right: [location? standing?]: this old bridge on the Miramichi is a silent witness to the Baptism in the waters below.

Below: Brown's Shipyard, Kent Co. (not standing): this bridge stood on the Richibucto River at the site of an old ship-yard.

PANB

Schwetz

Selected Bibliography

Allen, Richard Saunders. *Covered Bridges of the Northeast.* Revised edition, The Stephen Green Press, Brattleboro, Vermont, 1974.

Arbuckle, Doreen. *The North West Miramichi.* Printed by Westboro Printers Ltd., Ottawa, 1978.

Behind the Bushes. Volumes 1 & 2, Hendley Publishing Ltd., Fredericton, 1977.

Corbett, Scott. *Bridges.* Four Winds Press, New York, 1978.

Gies, Joseph. *Bridges and Men.* Doubleday and Company, Inc., Garden City, N.Y., 1963.

Harrington, Lyn and Richard. *Covered Bridges of Central and Eastern Canada.* McGraw Hill Ryerson Ltd., Montreal, 1976.

MacVey, C.A. *Correspondence: Bridge Department, Province of New Brunswick.* Public Archives of New Brunswick, Fredericton New Brunswick.

Journals of the New Brunswick Legislature: (1845) Tolls Saint Croix Bridge Corp.; (1889) Trotting Horses; (1926) Motor Vehicle Act; (1907) Abolition of Tolls On Hartland Bridge.

Index

Act of the Legislature (1845): 13
Adair Bridge: see North Becaguimec River No.1 (Carleton Co.)
Albert County Historical Society: 29
Albert Manufacturing Co.: 48
Alma Bridge: 92;   see Salmon River Mouth (Albert Co.)
angle block: 20
arched T-beam, 8
Arched-Burr Truss: 10
Armed Forces: see Camp Gagetown

Back Creek No.2: 70;   see Hoyt Station (Sunbury Co.)
Baker Brook No.2: 47;   see Morneault Settlement (Madawaska Co.)
Bamford Colpitts Bridge: see Coverdale River No.3
Baptism (on the Miramichi): 94
Barkers Point Bridge (York Co.): 63
Barnum, P.T.: 13
Base Gagetown: 52; Corps of Engineers
Bayard Bridge: see Nerepis River No.3 (Queens Co.)
Bay du Vin Bridge (Northumberland Co.): 37
Bayswater Bridge: see Milkish Inlet No.1 (Kings Co.)
Becaguimec River No.3: 26;   see Mangrum (Carleton Co.)
beech: 31
"Behind the Bushes": 52;   see League for Rural Renewal
Bell Bridge: see South Oromocto River No.3 (Sunbury Co.)
Bell Bridge: see Trout Creek No.3
Belleisle Creek No.2: 73;   see Marvin Bridge (Kings Co.)
Benton Bridge: see Eel River No.3

Big Salmon River Bridge (Saint John Co.): 82
Billings, Louella: 53
Black River Bridge (Northumberland Co.): 63
black spruce: 31, 61
Bloomfield Creek Bridge (Kings Co.): 57-8
Bloomfield School: 57
Boniface Bridge: see Green River No.3 (Madawaska Co.)
Boudreau Bridge: see Memramcook River No.4 (Westmorland Co.)
Brewer, Todd C.: 34
Bridge to Nowhere: see Ryan Bridge; Ryan, The Honorable P.G.
Bridge Supervisor: 38, 39 (Newcastle), 44
Brookton Bridge: 48
Brookton Road: 48
Brown's Shipyard Bridge (Kent Co.): 94
Budd Bridge: see Cocagne River No.5 (Westmorland Co.)
Bull Creek Bridge: 48, 49;   see Harris Steeves (Albert Co.)
Burnside Hayne Bridge: see Keswick River No.7 (York Co.)
Burnt Land Brook Bridge (Northumberland Co.): 84
Burpee Bridge: see Gaspereau River No.2 (Queens Co.)
Burpee, D.C.: 34
Burr (Bhurr), Theodore: 10
Burr Truss: 10, 45

Cain Bridge (Kings Co.): 27
Cameron Mill: see Kouchibouguacis No.5 (Kent Co.)
Canaan River No.1: 32;   see Clark Aaron Bridge (Queens Co.)
Canal Bridge (Charlotte Co.): 46
Carr, William C.: 62

cedar: 31
Centreville: see Millstream No.5; Pleasant Ridge Road (Kings Co.)
Chief Bridge Engineer: 28, 35, 38, 39, 61;   see C.A. MacVey, R.A. Molloy, B.H.
Hagerman, A.R. Wetmore
Chief Commissioner of Bridges: see The Honourable P.G. Ryan
Clark Aaron Bridge: see Canaan River No.1 (Queens Co.)
Cocagne River No.3: 20;   see Poirier Bridge (Westmorland Co.)
Cocagne River No.5: 78;   see Budd Bridge (Westmorland Co.)
Coles Island West Bridge (Queens Co.): 44
Colpitts, Bamford: see Coverdale Riv No.3; Bamford Colpitts Bridge
Colter Bridge: 52;   see Colter "Transplant"; League for Rural Renewal
Colter "Transplant": 50, 52, 53;   see Colter Bridge; League for Rural Renewal
Connors Bridge (Queens Co.): 29
Corps of Engineers: see Camp Gagetown
cottage roof: 29;   see hip roof
Coverdale River No.2: 17;   see John Mitton (Albert Co.)
Coverdale River No.3: 48, 49;   see Bamford Colpitts
Coverdale River No.7: 36;   see Tom Demille; Magnetic Hill; Parkingdale
Covered Bridge Society: 34
creosote: 31
Crooked Creek No.3: 69;   see Mouth Bridge (Albert Co.)

"Dance of Death Bridge": 9
Dan Cupid: see Hartley Steeves; Weldon Creek No.3 (Albert Co.)

Darlings Island Bridge (Kings Co.): 27
Dennis Stream: see Maxwell Crossing (Charlotte Co.)
Department of Agriculture: 50
Department of Health and Welfare: 50
Department of Public Works: 19, 26, 60
Department of Tourism: 50
Department of Transportation: 21, 52
Digdeguash River: 25
Digdeguash River No.2: 46;   see Stillwater (Charlotte Co.)
Digdeguash River No.3: 2;   see McGuire (Charlotte Co.)
Digdeguash River No.4: 44;   see McCann (Charlotte Co.)
Digdeguash River No.6: 68;   see Dumbarton (Charlotte Co.)
Doaktown: see Footbridge
Doaktown Historical Society: 30, 59;   see Nelson Hollow; Mill Brook No.1
Dodge: 48
Donald Bridge: see Upper Blackville Bridge (Northumberland Co.)
Douglas fir: 31, 61
Drummond Road: 28
Dumbarton Bridge: see Digdeguash River No.6 (Charlotte Co.)
Dysart, A.A.: 25, 40;   see Minister of Public Works

East Branch St. Nicholas River No. 1 (Kent Co.): 10
Eel River No.3: 64;   see Benton Bridge (York Co.)
Ellis Bridge: see North Becaguimec River No.4 (Carleton Co.)

Fawcett, W.R.: 34, 49
federal government: see Fundy National Park; Point Wolfe; Lower 45
Fernmount Bridge (Sunbury Co.): 86

Ferry Point Bridge: see Old Covered Bridge

Fletcher, R.C.: 61

Florence (Italy): see Ponte Vecchio

Florenceville (Carleton Co.): 35

Florenceville Bridge (Carleton Co.): 35

Flume Ridge Bridge: see Magaguadavic River No.7

Footbridge, Doaktown: 13

Forks Bridge: see Richardson Bridge (Queens Co.)

French Village Bridge: see Hammond River No.2 (Kings Co.)

Fundy National Park: 7, 40; see Point Wolfe; Lower 45

Gaspereau River: 15

Gaspereau River No.2: 15; see Burpee Bridge (Queens Co.)

Germantown Lake Bridge: see Shepody River No.3

Gill Bridge (Northumberland Co.): 93

Godin, Patrich: 40

Goshen Road: see Malone Bridge; Kennebecasis River No.3 (Kings Co.)

Goulette, Joseph and John: 34

Graham Creek Bridge: 40; see Tom Graham Bridge (Kent Co.)

Green, Fred: 35

Green River No.3: 32; see Boniface Bridge (Madawaska Co.)

Ground Hog Day Gale: see Narrows Bridge

Gunningsville Bridge: 7

Haggerman, B.H.: 8; see Chief Bridge Engineer

Haines, Alfred: 15

Hammond River No.2: 71; see French Village (Kings Co.)

Hammond River No.3: 10; see Smithtown (Kings Co.)

Hardscrabble Bridge: see Vaughan Creek No.2 (Saint John Co.)

Harris Steeves Bridge: see Bull Creek (Albert Co.)

Hartley Steeves: see Dan Cupid; Weldon Creek No.3 (Albert Co.)

Hartland Bridge (Carleton Co.): 14, 60-2

Hartland Toll Bridge Company: 60, 62

Hasty Bridge: see Petitcodiac River No.3 (Westmorland Co.)

Hawkes Bridge (Kings Co.): 85

hemlock: 31

Hexham (Northumberland Co.): 35

High Marsh Road: see Tantramar River No.2; Wheaton

Highways Act: 38, 39; see snowing bridges

Highways Department: 7

Historical Resources Administration: 50

hip roof: 14, 29, 59, 80; see cottage roof

Hirons, Charles: 35

"horsebacks": 31

horses (trotting): 15

Howe Truss: 10, 20, 29, 45, 55, 61, 62

Howe, William: 10

Hoyt Station: see Back Creek No.2 (Sunbury Co.)

Hughes, P.: 18, 34

Hunters Ferry (Queens Co.): 82

Irish River: see Vaughan Creek No.1 (Saint John Co.)

Iroquois River No.4 (Madawaska Co.): 43

Joshua Gallant Bridge: see Shediac River No.4 (Westmorland Co.)

Jumbo: 13

Keenan Bridge: see Monquart River No.3 (Carleton Co.)

Kennebecasis River No.3: 22; see Malone Bridge; Goshen Road

Kennebecasis River No.8: 34; see Salmon Bridge

Kennebecasis River No.9: 23, 50; see Plumweseep; League for Rural Renewal

Kent Parish (Carleton Co.): 36

Keswick River No.6: 74; see Stone Ridge (York Co.)

Keswick River No.7: cover, 30, 47; see Burnside Haines [Hayne] (York Co.)

king post: 9, 10

king truss: 37

King Street: see Ryan Brook Mouth; Oak Hall

Kouchibouguacis No.5: 45; see Cameron Mill (Kent Co.)

Landry, Alfred M.: 40

Landry, F.: 40

Landry, Leo M.: 40

League for Rural Renewal: 21, 50, 52, 78; New Horizons Program

Lester Bridge (Kings Co.): 87

Light, Alex L.: 33

Linton Bridge (Charlotte Co.): 92

Little Lepreau River No.1: 21; see Mill Pond (Charlotte Co.)

Lockhart Mills (Carleton Co.): see Shikatehawk River No.2

Logan, R.A.: 34

Long Creek No.1: 39; see Starkey Bridge (Queens Co.)

Lovely, John: 35

Lower Forty-Five No.1: 7

Lucerne (Switzerland): see "Dance of Death Bridge"

MacFarlane Bridge: see Wards Creek No.2

MacVey, C.A.: 6, 22, 61; see Chief Bridge Engineer

Magaguadavic River No.7: 45; see Flume Ridge (Charlotte Co.)

Magnetic Hill Bridge: 5, 21, 36; see Coverdale River No.7 (Tom Demille)

Malloy, R.A.: 8; see Chief Bridge Engineer

Malloy, R.B.: 8

Malone: see Kennebecasis River No.3, Goshen Road (Kings Co.)

Mangrum Bridge: see Becaguimec River No.3 (Carleton Co.)

maple: 31

Marysville Bridge (York Co.): 81

Matchett, Garfield: 55

Marvin Bridge: see Belleisle Creek No.2 (Kings Co.)

Maxwell Crossing: 42; see Dennis Stream (Charlotte Co.)

McBride Bridge (Carleton Co.): 37

McCann Bridge: 25; see Digdeguash River No.4 (Charlotte Co.)

McConnell Bridge (Westmorland Co.): 93

McGuire Bridge: see Digdeguash River No.3 (Charlotte Co.)

McLaggen & Boone: 34

Meanen Cove Bridge (Kings Co.): 19

Memramcook River No.4: 77; see Boudreau Bridge (Westmorland Co.)

Milkish Inlet No.1: 43; see Bayswater Bridge (Kings Co.)

Mill Brook No.1: 30, 59; see Nelson Hollow (Northumberland Co.)

Mill Creek Bridge: 26

Mill Pond: see Little Lepreau River No.1 (Charlotte Co.)

Mill Settlement: see South Oromocto River No.2 (Sunbury Co.)

Millstream No.5: 24; see Centreville (Kings Co.)

Milltown Dam Bridge (Charlotte Co.): 88

Minister of Bridge Dept.: 17, 18, 38; see T.B. Winslow

Minister of Public Works: 26, 44; see P.J. Veniot, A.A. Dysart

Mitton, John (Albert Co.): see Coverdale River No.2

Model Farm Road: 19

Moncton: 5, 21

Monquart River No.3: 73; see Keenan (Carleton Co.)

Moores Mill Bridge: see Trout Creek No.5 (Kings Co.)

Moosehorn Creek Bridge: 21; see James Neales

Morneault Settlement: see Baker Brook No.2 (Madawaska Co.)

Motor Vehicle Branch: 39

Motor Vehicle Law, 1926: 16

Mouth Bridge (1): see Crooked Creek No.3 (Albert Co.)

Mouth Bridge (2): see St. Nicholas River No.1 (Kent Co.)

Mouth Bridge (3): see Salmon River; Alma (Albert Co.)

Mouth Bridge (4): see Tynemouth Creek Bridge (Saint John Co.)

Nackawic River No.5: 14; see Nackawic Siding (York Co.)

Nackawic Siding Bridge: see Nackawic River No.5 (York Co.)

Narrows Bridge (Queens Co.): 42

Nashwaak Valley: 24

National Parks of Canada: 41

Navigable Waters Protection Act: 43; see Bayswater Bridge; Milkish Inlet No.1

Neales, Connie: 57

Neales [Neals], James: 21, 62

Nelson Hollow Bridge: 14, 29, 47; see Mill Brook No.1 (Northumberland Co.)

Nerepis River No.3: 67; see Bayard Bridge (Queens Co.)

Newcastle: 39

New England: 10

New Horizons Program: 50; see League for Rural Renewal

Newtown: see Oldfield Bridge; Smith Creek No.5 (Kings Co.)

North Becaguimec River No.1: 47, 68; see Adair (Carleton Co.)

North Becaguimec River No.4: 47; see Ellis (Carleton Co.)

North Branch Bridge: 9; see Plaster Rock-Renous Highway (North)

Northwest Miramichi: see Red Bank Bridge

Norton (Kings Co.): 33

Notre-Dame Bridge (Kent Co.): 80

oak: 31

Oak Hall: see Ryan Brook Mouth Bridge

Odellach River No.2: 8; see Tomlinson Mill (Victoria Co.)

Old Covered Bridge (St. Stephen): 13; see Ferry Point Bridge

Oldfield: see Smith Creek No.5, Newtown (Kings Co.)

open-faced cribwork: 26

Palladio, Andrea: 9-10

Parkingdale: see Coverdale No.7; Riverview Bridge

Park Bridge: see Point Wolfe

Patrick Owen Bridge: 50; see Rusagonis River No.2; League for Rural Renewal

patronage: 25

Peter Jonah Bridge: 29; see Turtle Creek No.4 (Albert Co.)

Petitcodiac River No.3: 12; see Hasty Bridge (Westmorland Co.)

Picadilly Bridge: see Urney; Trout Creek No.4 (Kings Co.)

Plaster Rock (unnamed bridge): 87

Plaster Rock-Renous Highway: see North Branch Bridge

Pleasant Ridge Road: see Millstream No.5; Centreville (Kings Co.)

Plumweseep Bridge: see Kennebecasis River No.9; League for Rural Renewal

Point Wolfe Bridge (Albert Co.): 40, 41

Poirier Bridge: see Cocagne River No.3 (Westmorland Co.)

Ponte Vecchio: 9

Porter Cove Bridge (Northumberland Co.): 81

Powers Construction Company: 61; see Hartland Bridge

Puget Sound: 16

purlin: 31

Queen post: 9

queen truss: 9

Quisibis River No.2: 47, 75; see Theriault Settlement (Madawaska Co.)

R.C.M.P.: 35

Red Bank No. 3 (Northumberland Co.): 54, 55-7

Red Bank No 4 (Northumberland Co.): 55

Red Bank Bridge (Queens Co.): 89

Reid Brothers (Gagetown): 39

Renton, Austin: 36; see Magnetic Hill Bridge

Rialto: 9

Richardson Bridge: 80; see Forks Bridge (Queens Co.)

"riprap": 26

Riverview Bridge (Parkingdale, Albert Co.): 90

Robertson and Hackett Sawmill Co.: 31

Rollingdam: 25

Rollingdam Bridge: 25

Rothesay Fire Dept.: 19

Rural Development: 50

Rusagonis River No.2: 5, 6, 50; see Patrick Owen

Ryan Bridge (Kings Co.): 85

Ryan Bridge (York Co.): 48; see "Bridge to Nowhere"; Ryan, The Honourable P.G.

Ryan Brook Mouth Bridge (Kings Co.): 84

Ryan, The Honourable P.G.: 15, 48, 85; see Chief Commissioner of Bridges

Sackville Bridge: 33

Saint Croix Bridge Corporation: 13

Salmon Bridge: see Kennebecasis River No.8 (Kings Co.)

Salmon River Mouth Bridge: see Alma (Albert Co.)

Saint John: 26

Saint Martins: 19

Saint Nicholas River No.1: 71; see Mouth (Kent Co.)

Salmon River Bridge: see Kennebecasis River No.8 (Kings Co.)

Saw Mill Creek No.1: 18

Second Falls Bridge (Charlotte Co.): 91

Sharp Bridge (Kings Co.): 86

Shediac River (Mouth) Bridge (Westmorland Co.): 39

Shediac River No.4: 76; see Joshua Gallant (Westmorland Co.)

Shepody River No.3: 12; see Germantown Lake Bridge

Shikatehawk River No.2: 36; see Lockhart Mill (Carleton Co.)

ship knees: 32, 33

Simmons, C.J.B.: 34

Smith Creek No.1: 2;   see Tranton Bridge (Kings Co.)

Smith Creek No.5: 15;   see Oldfield Bridge, Newtown (Kings Co.)

Smithtown Bridge: see Hammond River No.3 (Kings Co.)

Smye, Albert E.: 17, 18, 34, 41, 92

snowing the bridge: see Highways Act

South Canaan Road: see Clark Aaron Bridge; Canaan River No.1

South Oromocto River No.2: 74;   see Mill Settlement (Sunbury Co.)

South Oromocto River No.3: 8;   see Bell Bridge (Sunbury Co.)

Starkey Bridge: 48;   see Long Creek No.1; W.M. Starkey

Starkey, W.M.: 48;   see Starkey Bridge; Long Creek No.1

Stillwater: see Digdeguash River No.2

Stone Ridge Bridge: see Keswick River No.6 (York Co.)

Strutted Burr: 10

Tacoma Narrows Bridge: 15-16

Tantramar River No.2: 16;   see Wheaton Bridge (Westmorland Co.)

tendering: 17, 34

Theriault Settlement Bridge: see Quisibis River No.2

Tingley, Mariner M.: 34

Titus Bridge (Kings Co.): 91

Tom Demille Bridge: see Magnetic Hill; Coverdale River No.7

Tom Graham Bridge: see Graham Bridge (Kent Co.)

Tomlinson Mill: see Odellach River No.2 (Victoria Co.)

Town, Ithiel: 10

Town Truss: 10, 31

Town Lattice: 10

Tranton Bridge: see Smith Creek No.1 (Kings Co.)

Travelling Bridge: see William Mitton Bridge

Treatise on Architecture: 9

Trout Creek No.3: 78;   see Bell Bridge (Kings Co.)

Trout Creek No.4: 51;   see Picadilly; Urney (Kings Co.)

Trout Creek No.5: 28;   see Moores Mill (Kings Co.)

truss: 9, 15

Turtle Creek No.4: 14, 29;   see Peter Jonah (Albert Co.)

Tynemouth Creek Bridge: 7;   see Mouth Bridge (Saint John Co.)

United Empire Loyalists: 10

Upper Blackville Bridge: 83;   see Donald Bridge (Northumberland Co.)

Upper Dorchester Bridge (Westmorland Co.): 89

Upper Jemseg Bridge (Queens Co.): 25

Up-Set End: 10

Urney Bridge: see Picadilly; Trout Creek No.4 (Kings Co.)

U.S.Army Engineers: see Colter "Transplant"

Vaughan Creek No.1: 19;   see Irish River (Saint John Co.)

Vaughan Creek No.2: 19;   see Hardscrabble; Saint Martins (Saint John Co.)

Venice: see Rialto

Veniot, P.J.:   see Minister of Public Works

Wallace Blakeny Bridge (Westmorland Co.): 90

Wane Edge: 33

Wards Creek No.2: 72;   see MacFarlane Bridge (Kings Co.)

Webb Member: 20

Weldon Creek No.3: back cover, 49;   see Hartley Steeves; Dan Cupid (Albert Co.)

Wetmore, A.R.: 7, 48;   see Chief Bridge Engineer

William Mitton Bridge: 37, 38;   see Travelling Bridge (Albert Co.)

Wheaton Bridge: see Tantramar River No.2 (Westmorland Co.)

white pine: 31

Whitman Bros.: 18

Winslow, T.B.: 18, 34;   see Minister of Bridge Dept.

Wolfe, General: see Point Wolfe, Fundy National Park

Women's Institute: 50

yellow birch: 31

99

Ron Badger

Ruth Bay

Like his brother John, Stephen Gillis was born within sight of the old Red Bank Covered Bridge on the Main Nor' West Miramichi but the bridge was destroyed by fire in 1953 when he was aged two. One of Stephen's earliest memories is of crossing the ice bridge from Red Bank to Sunny Corner during the following winters.

A schoolteacher by occupation, Stephen enjoyed the challenge of finding, photographing, and researching the old bridges. Many a trek down dusty roads in hot weather, with a car-load of cranky kids and a frazzled wife, eventually resulted in this publication.

John Gillis was born in the village of Red Bank on the banks of the Miramichi in 1956. Trained in the delicate art of photography by the Armed Forces of Canada and by his own initiative, he is now a practising member of the Professional Photographers of Canada and lives and works in Toronto.

John's Northumberland County birthplace was once home to many covered bridges crossing an abundance of streams and rivers. The last one stands today in Nelson Hollow near Doaktown.

101

EAST

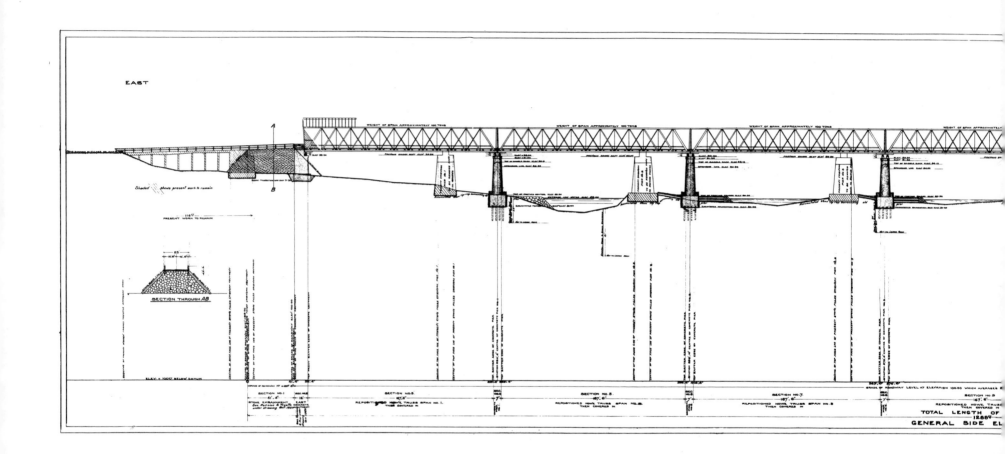

Shaded ▨ shows present work to remain

← 116'0" →
PRESENT WORK TO REMAIN

SECTION THROUGH AB

WEIGHT OF SPAN APPROXIMATELY 100 TONS   WEIGHT OF SPAN APPROXIMATELY 100 TONS   WEIGHT OF SPAN APPROXIMATELY 100 TONS   WEIGHT OF SPAN APPROXIMATELY

SECTION NO.1   SECTION NO.3   SECTION NO.5   SECTION NO.7   SECTION NO.9

STONE EMBANKMENT   REPOSITIONED HOWE TRUSS SPAN NO.1   REPOSITIONED HOWE TRUSS SPAN NO.2   REPOSITIONED HOWE TRUSS SPAN NO.3   REPOSITIONED HOWE TRUS
                   THEN COVERED IN   THEN COVERED IN   THEN COVERED IN   THEN COVERED IN

GRADE OF ROADWAY LEVEL AT ELEVATION 100.00 WHICH AVERAGES

TOTAL LENGTH OF
12884'
GENERAL SIDE EL